Mainely Kids

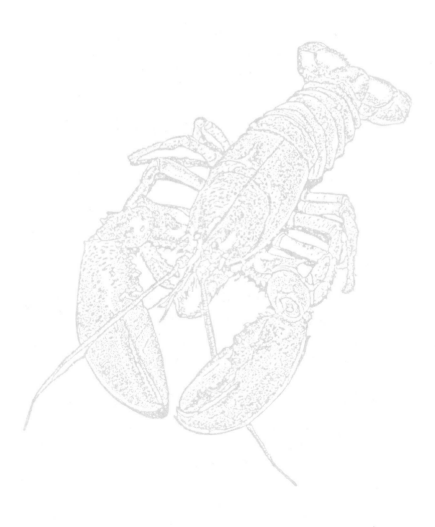

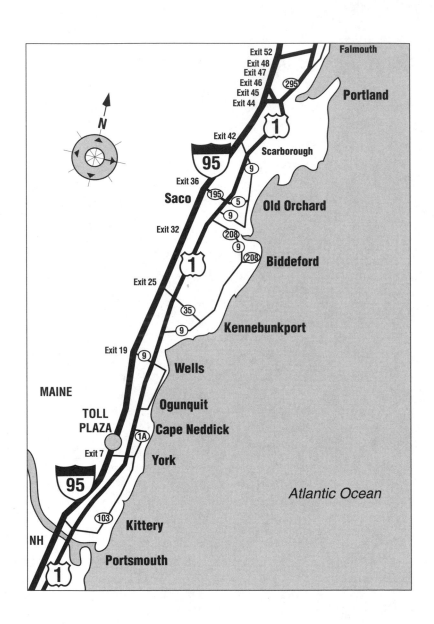

Mainely Kids

A GUIDE TO FAMILY FUN IN SOUTHERN MAINE

CRYSTAL WARD KENT

University Press of New England
Hanover and London

Published by University Press of New England,

One Court Street, Lebanon, NH 03766

www.upne.com

©2006 by Crystal Ward Kent

Printed in the United States of America

5   4   3   2   1

Library of Congress Cataloging-in-Publication Data
Kent, Crystal Ward.
    Mainely kids : a guide to family fun in southern Maine /
Crystal Ward Kent.
        p.   cm.
    Includes index.
    ISBN-13: 978-1-58465-552-7 (paperback : alk. paper)
    ISBN-10: 1-58465-552-6 (paperback : alk. paper)
    1. Maine—Guidebooks. 2. Family recreation—Maine—Guidebooks.
    3. Children—Travel—Maine—Guidebooks.   I. Title.
    F17.3.K46   2006
    917.41'0444—dc22   2006001965

Unless otherwise indicated, photographs are by the author.

Frontispiece: Map of southern coast. From Route 95 North or Route 1
North, you can access a wealth of activities in scenic southern Maine.
Map by Denise Brown of Ad-Cetera Graphics.

This book is dedicated to my family. Thank you for your support! Special thanks to Marcia Peverly, my friend and colleague. Marcia's vast expertise on the state and its attractions was of invaluable help when I was preparing this book.

Crystal Ward Kent—July 2005

Contents

About the Information in *Mainely Kids*

As this book went to press, the information was accurate. However, just like the weather, things change along the coast of Maine. Businesses change names and owners. Some close; new ones open. Policies change regarding use of beaches and parks. Attractions may change their focus, and traditional events give way to new ones, or hours and seasons may be altered. Before you plan your vacation around a particular attraction or event, call to make sure it is still around. "Know before you go" is still a good rule of thumb!

Your best bet for verifying information is the Maine Tourism Association. Call their main office in Kittery at (207) 439-1319. They can answer questions or send information to help you plan your trip. You can also stop by on your way into Maine to pick up a wealth of brochures, maps, and booklets. Their facility in Kittery is accessible from both Interstate 95 North and U.S. Route 1 North.

Other invaluable resources are the local chambers of commerce and visitor centers. The phone numbers for the chambers or visitor centers for each community are found in each chapter of this book. Phone numbers for specific attractions and events, where applicable, are also included.

Overview

Before You Go

Welcome to Maine! Maine is a great family vacation destination because of the diversity of activities available. Beautiful sandy beaches, rocky shores and lighthouses, tidepooling, and whale-watching all await you. Visit one of our historic villages and step back in time to the 1800s. Live the life of long ago as you assume the role of an actual villager from that period. Learn the gruesome legend of Boon Island; take a ghostly tour of Olde York, clamber about a fort perched high on a windy bluff. Take a walk on the wild side and explore our many nature preserves. Watch a lobsterman haul in his catch or spend a day on the ocean fishing for your own supper. Swing high on a ferris wheel at Old Orchard Beach, one of the country's oldest and most famous amusement centers, or hurtle down the biggest slide in the water park. All these things and more are found in southern Maine.

Mainely Kids is designed to help you plan the family vacation you want by providing ideas for fun activities in this part of the state. Each chapter visits a different area and notes the natural, historical, and family attractions found there. There are also ideas for fun things to do that you might not have considered, such as good places for kite flying or seeing wildlife, where to sample traditional Maine food, or where to hear about local ghosts. The book also includes some interesting facts about the state's history, flora and fauna, and items uniquely Maine.

Before you visit, there are a few things you should know. If you plan to arrive in the summer, be prepared for Maine's changeable climate. One day can be hot and sunny, while the next can be quite cool. Evening temperatures also can be significantly lower than daytime ones. The greatest weather changes occur along the coast and in the mountains. You will have a more enjoyable vacation if you pack accordingly. Along with those swimsuits and shorts, include sweatshirts, sweaters, jackets, rain slickers, long pants, and outdoor boots. This way, no matter what the weather or temperature, you are prepared and can enjoy your vacation in comfort.

And, don't forget the sunscreen! Although Maine has a cooler summer climate than many states, the sun is still beaming down upon you and can easily cause a painful burn. If you are boating, at the beach, or in the water, the effects are magnified. Remember to "lather up" with protective lotion and wear a hat.

Another "must-bring" is bug spray. Maine has a booming population of mosquitoes, black flies, ticks, and other biting insects. If you plan to spend time outdoors hiking or camping, bring insect repellent for your comfort and protection. Lyme disease (carried by deer ticks) does exist in Maine, so use the bug spray. For even better protection in deep woods, wear long sleeves, pants tucked into boots, and a hat, and perform regular "tick checks" on each other.

Many of the fun things to do in southern Maine are outdoor hikes. You will have a more meaningful experience if you bring or buy some field guides to local birds or animals. These will help you identify tracks and calls, as well as any wildlife you might see. A good pair of binoculars is also a great asset on a hike.

And don't forget the camera! Maine is known for its scenery, so whether you are dazzled by an ocean sunset, the charm of a fishing village, or a glimpse of wildlife, you may want to capture it on film. Pictures are among the least expensive souvenirs you can bring back from your trip, yet can be the most memorable. These days, children can easily enjoy picture taking by using a disposable camera. The quality is good; the camera cost is usually reasonable; and this way, everyone can snap up their memories of Maine. (If you forgot to bring one, nearly any pharmacy or retail store will have them for sale.) You might also consider creating a travel journal with your children. Encourage them to jot down their impressions or favorite experiences, add drawings, or paste in brochures and postcards. A simple spiral notebook will work just fine, and it is an easy way to create a unique memento of your trip.

Most of the outdoor activities mentioned in this book are possible from mid-May to October. If you are visiting earlier or later than those months, you may find outdoor activity hindered by snow, ice, or cold.

Please note that most attractions, such as theme parks, are not open until early June, and frequently close near Labor Day. More details on typical season dates are offered in the upcoming section. Specific information on individual attractions is included in the regional chapters.

Maine has one major highway artery into the state—Interstate 95, also called the Maine Turnpike. Consequently, on popular summer or fall weekends, traffic can be very heavy northbound on Friday evenings and Saturday mornings, and southbound on Sunday evenings. If you do not wish to sit in slow-moving traffic with children, you might consider planning your vacation travel during the week, or on a Thursday to Sunday morning.

As you read this book, please note that for the most part, each chapter takes you on a circular loop of activities found in that region. Directions to each attraction are noted as they would be found along the loop. For directions directly to that attraction from your home area, visit the web site or call that attraction directly.

While much of the book focuses on the southern coast, the last two chapters focus on some interesting inland attractions, and also talk about fun activities that are found throughout Maine. Pick-your-own farm stands, agricultural fairs, miniature golfing—these are just a few of the fun things that can be done throughout Maine and should definitely be enjoyed while you are here.

To explore the entire southern coastal region ideally would take a week or two. However, any one of the areas listed in the individual chapters can be enjoyed in a long weekend.

We hope this book proves helpful. Enjoy Maine and your vacation!

About Handicapped Accessibility

Handicapped accessibility is still a tricky subject in Maine. As this book went to press, existing attractions were not required to become fully handicapped accessible if it meant major changes. Gray areas also surround exactly what is considered handicapped accessible and what is not. For example, parks such as Fort Foster in Kittery list themselves as handicapped accessible, and they are in terms of access to the park itself, getting to picnic areas, and even walking some of the trails (trails are fairly level, although dirt or gravel). However, the bathrooms would have difficulty accommodating a wheelchair.

Most major attractions, such as York's Wild Kingdom in York, Funtown/Splashtown in Saco, and Palace Playland in Old Orchard Beach, are handicapped accessible.

Most shops and restaurants are handicapped accessible.

Many nature reserves would be questionable—you may be able to enter the park and even access some of the trails, but many do not have accommodating facilities beyond that. (Many have no facilities at all!)

In other cases, there are pleasant surprises, as even some smaller fishing boats can accommodate those with physical disabilities. The *Deborah Ann* out of Ogunquit is one such craft.

The situation on handicapped accessibility continues to change as owners change, regulations change, and awareness changes.

If you require handicapped accessibility, it is wise to call the individual attraction or park you wish to visit, or barring the availability of a phone (in the case of some parks or beaches), to contact the local chamber.

About the Maps in this Book

The maps provided in this book are accurate but greatly simplified. They do not include every street and road in the areas depicted. They do encompass the main routes needed for you to get to the attractions and sights mentioned in this book, and also give you a sense of the area. If you wish more detailed maps, stop at the local chamber or the Maine Tourism Association.

About Activity Fees and Restaurant Prices

Most of the activities mentioned in this book are very affordable for a family of four. Many of the natural attractions have no fee at all. The more costly items will be the commercial attractions such as amusement parks. However, even these offer a variety of options to choose from in terms of ticket packages and discounts based on time of day, time of year, or special events.

If you are coming to Maine, most likely you and your family will want to sample some delicious Maine lobster or other seafood. In general, any seafood restaurant will have a wide range of offerings and something will be suitable for a family's budget. Chowders, fish and chips, and other casual food are usually very affordable. Even clams are offered in a range of sizes (a basket versus a plate), and lobsters come in different sizes and are sold by the pound. If you want to try lobster, but blanch at the price of a full-size steamed one, try a lobster roll. There is something for every pocketbook.

Be advised that prices for lobster and other seafood, such as clams, vary greatly each season, and with time of year. (Lobsters move farther offshore during winter, making them more costly to trap as boats have to go out farther.) Cost is dependent on whether the harvest was good, market demand, and other factors. For example, if a "red tide" occurs during the summer months, causing clam flats to be closed for extended periods, then clam prices will be high due to scarcity of the product. Red tide is a naturally occurring "bloom" or population explosion of microscopic plankton that can affect shellfish such as clams. Cooking does not kill the toxins emitted by the plankton. If people eat clams that are diseased by red tide, they can suffer paralytic shellfish poisoning that, although rare, can be fatal. Clam flats are rigorously monitored for any signs of red tide and professional shellfishermen check consistently to make sure that flats are safe for harvesting. Likewise, conscientious restaurants are careful to buy shellfish from reputable sources. If you have concerns about the safety of shellfish, don't hesitate to ask where it came from and when. You can also call the Shellfish Sanitation Hotline at 1-800-232-4733 to check on red tide and pollution flat closures.

The prices for other seafood can also be affected by a variety of factors. If the winter and spring have been stormy, fishing boats may have suffered extensive losses of gear, and been unable to venture out as frequently. Catches will then be down, and the market will reflect higher prices.

Because of these variables, which can greatly affect prices, no attempts have been made to estimate the costs of lobster, clams, or other seafood in this book. They will vary according to the season, the restaurant, and natural factors.

About Safe Hiking

Many of the activities suggested in this book are hikes. Most would be short day hikes, but even so, one should always be prepared. Every year, hundreds of hikers get lost in the Maine woods. Most are found okay, usually because they were prepared and had some survival skills.

Whenever you are hiking, especially with small children, be sure to carry a few basic survival items. One wrong turn can turn a short day hike into being lost for several hours, or worse. Being prepared can make the difference between being uncomfortable or becoming seriously ill.

Always carry water, snacks, basic first aid supplies, a survival blanket, any medications you must have, flashlight, matches, and a knife. The silver, thermal survival blankets fold down to thin squares and can be purchased at most any store carrying outdoor goods. Because of their silvery color, they can also be used for signaling. Regarding medications, if your child is an asthmatic, for example, always have his or her rescue inhaler with you. If you or your children have severe allergies (such as to bee stings), obtain a prescription Epipen for use in case of anaphylactic shock and have it in your pack. A cell phone is not necessarily your most reliable tool. In many areas, you will not be able to get reception, and a cell phone will not keep you warm or quench your thirst.

Be sure you know basic first aid before venturing into a wild area. The American Red Cross offers courses regularly. The Red Cross also sometimes offers survival courses. Many outdoor outfitters have courses, or can put you in touch with a class. At the least, know how to make a fire and build a shelter of pine boughs (or snow in winter).

If you do become lost, stay put. Searchers will keep narrowing the search grid and will eventually find you. It is much harder to track a moving target.

Always check in at the ranger station or with personnel at the reserve before going on a hike. This way, if you don't return, someone knows you are missing.

About Season Dates

What is "the" season? For most commercial attractions, the season is typically Memorial Day to Labor Day. However, with town and state parks, the season may vary. These parks are usually open Memorial Day to Labor Day, but some may also take advantage of the nice fall weather and be open, at least on weekends, into mid- or late October. Others may have their gates open during the week in foliage season, and not charge fees, but have no facilities available, or only limited facilities. Still others may allow access in winter for cross-country skiing or snowshoeing, but require you to park outside the gate. No facilities would be open under these circumstances and no fees would be charged. If you plan to visit a park during a possibly off-season time, your best bet is to check the web site before you go, or ask locally. This way you can be sure about what facilities are available and if any fees are being charged.

Tourism is one of Maine's biggest businesses and if good weather allows, many businesses may extend their hours beyond the typical season. For example, if summer-like weather seems to be extending into September or even early October, beach area shops, attractions such as miniature golf, and historic homes may extend their season for several weeks into the fall and be open at least on weekends. By the same token, if the weather after Labor Day is cold and rainy, many of these activities will begin to close. Similarly, if spring is warm and sunny, a few attractions may open before Memorial Day, at least on the weekends. If the spring is cold, openings may be delayed until the first weekend or two in June. It is wise to call ahead if you are visiting in spring or fall. This way, you will not be disappointed if an opening date is delayed, or an attraction has closed early.

About Traffic Laws

For a handbook of Maine traffic laws, contact the Maine State Department of Motor Vehicles at (207) 624-9000 (under Secretary of State). Some key laws that may differ from your state are these: (1) Seatbelts are required for everyone, not just for children; (2) A right turn on a red light is allowed after a complete stop, unless posted otherwise; and (3) no helmet is required for adult motorcyclists, although some restrictions do apply. Children under age fifteen are required to wear a helmet; all passengers, whether riding on the back of the motorcycle or in a sidecar, are required to wear a helmet; and anyone driving a motorcycle with a learner's permit must wear protective headgear.

About Maine

Maine is the largest of the five New England States. It is 320 miles long and 210 miles wide, with a total land area of 33,215 square miles, making it as big as all the other New England states combined.

Maine consists of 16 counties with 22 cities, 424 towns, 51 plantations, and 416 unorganized townships. (Townships and plantations are very small communities with no official governing bodies.) Maine has one county (Aroostook, also known as "The County") so big (6,453 square miles) that it covers an area greater than the combined states of Connecticut and Rhode Island.

Maine is blessed with 6,000 lakes and ponds, 32,000 miles of rivers and streams, 17 million acres of forestland, more than 5,000 miles of coastline, and 2,000 islands. The state abounds in natural assets, with 542,629 acres of state and national parks, including the 92-mile Allagash Wilderness Waterway, Acadia National Park (the second-most-visited national park in the United States), and Baxter State Park, which is the home of Mount Katahdin and the northern end of the Appalachian Trail. The Appalachian Trail originates in Georgia and follows the Appalachian Mountain chain along the eastern seaboard. Mount Katahdin is the only mountain in the state that soars one mile in height, rising 5,268 feet above sea level.

Acadia National Park is located on Mount Desert Island, which is also home to Bar Harbor, one of the state's most popular tourist destinations. The park is about two-thirds up the Maine coast.

Baxter State Park and Mount Katahdin are located in the northern third of the state in an area called the "Maine Highlands." Moosehead Lake is also found within this region. Bangor, the gateway city to the Highlands, is home to acclaimed novelist Stephen King.

Maine claims America's first chartered city, York, which was incorporated in 1641, and 65 lighthouses, stretching from Kittery in the south to Quoddy Head in easternmost Washington County. These include Portland Head Light, which was commissioned by George Washington.

Agriculture still plays a prominent role in Maine's economy, with potatoes, poultry, blueberries, and apples among the top crops. Maine is America's largest wild blueberry growing state, raising 98 percent of the lowbush blueberry crop in the United States. Logging, for timber and pulp and paper, is still a primary industry.

Maine is also internationally known for its shellfish, averaging nearly 40 million pounds of lobster harvested annually. The combined total of all shellfish (lobsters, clams, etc.) and finfish harvested annually is more than 200 million pounds. Among finfish, the top catches are Atlantic salmon, sea herring, flounder-dab, and angler-monkfish. Among shellfish, lobster tops the list, followed by shrimp and scallops. Sea urchins are also a top crop.

Facts about Maine

✳ **State Nickname:** The Pine Tree State

✳ **State Capital:** Augusta

✳ **Population:** Approximately 1.2 million

✳ **State Animal:** The moose

✳ **State Tree:** The white pine

✳ **State Gemstone:** Tourmaline

✳ **State Insect:** The honey bee

✳ **State Bird:** The black-capped chickadee

✳ **State Fish:** Landlocked salmon

✳ **State Herb:** Wintergreen

✳ **State Cat:** Maine coon cat

✳ **State Fossil:** *Pertica quadrifaria* (This vascular land plant may have reached heights of 6 feet. It grew 390 million years ago in brackish areas or freshwater marshes on recently created volcanic soil in what is now Quebec and New Brunswick, Canada, Maine, and Norway.)

✳ **State Motto:** Dirigo ("I lead")

✳ **State Song:** "State of Maine Song"

Mainely Kids

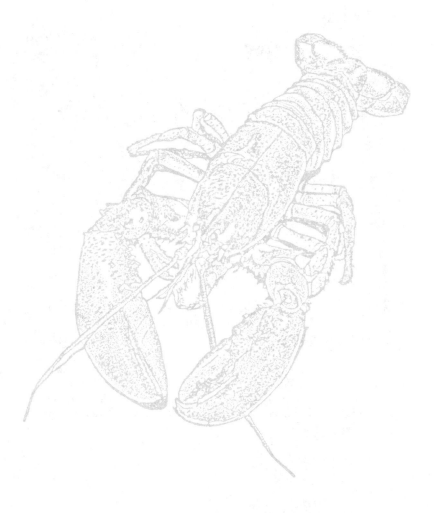

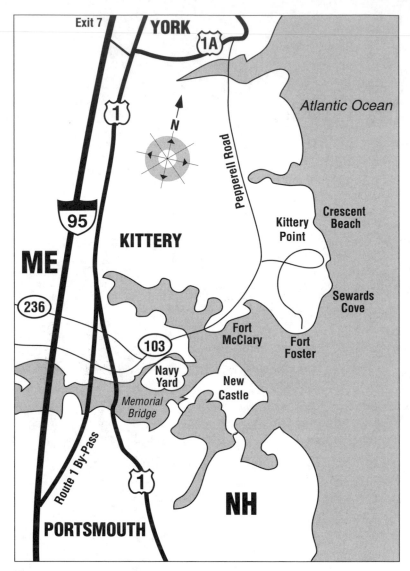

Kittery

Kittery is the "Gateway to Maine." Be sure to visit Fort McClary and Fort Foster for a taste of history and great shore walks, and Frisbee's General Store for a glimpse of old-time Maine. *Map by Denise Brown of Ad-Cetera Graphics.*

In and around Kittery and Kittery Point, discover Fort Foster, Fort McClary, and unspoiled beaches for tidepooling, swimming, and exploring. You will also find some good places to fish and hike, fly kites and picnic, eat lobster and watch lobstering. The outlet malls and the Kittery Trading Post are additional stops recommended in this chapter.

Kittery is where Maine begins. Called the "Gateway," it is the state's oldest community and the geographical entry point to the southern part of the state. Settlers arrived on Kittery's shores in 1623 and the town was incorporated in 1652. Fishing, shipbuilding, and farming were its original economic mainstays. Today, shipbuilding and fishing remain, but retail ventures have pushed past farming as a livelihood. Kittery, however, still maintains much of its small-town charm. Old clapboard houses march right down to a shoreline still heavily dotted with fishing piers. Gulls wheel about, and boats ride at anchor, waiting the call of the sea.

Kittery and Kittery Point both offer many family activities, though little in the way of attractions. To get some sense of the real Kittery, spend a few hours at the Piscataqua River and watch the activity around the **Memorial Bridge.** It may seem like an odd suggestion, but the bridge and the river are the heartbeat of the region. The Memorial Bridge is one of two working drawbridges on the Piscataqua River. It connects Portsmouth, New Hampshire, to Kittery, Maine, and was built in 1919 as a tribute to World War I soldiers. Before it was built, those wishing to cross from rural Maine to the city of Portsmouth had to row over—no mean feat given that the Piscataqua River is the second-fastest river in the country. (The second drawbridge, the Sarah Long or Route 1 Bypass Bridge, is further up the river.) Just watching the river is mesmerizing: It literally races by, seething with tidepools, eddies, and its own swift current. Those who have tried to swim it have wound up a half mile off course—that is, those who did not need to be rescued!

During summer, the bridge rises every half hour to allow boat traffic to proceed up and down the river. Ships send a signal to the bridge, a siren rings, gates come down to block traffic, and the bridge operators swing into action. Slowly, the central section of the bridge is raised and the boats begin to come through. All kinds of exciting craft go by. On any given day, you may see sailboats, fishing boats, pleasure boats, big tankers, salt ships (ships bringing huge cargoes of salt which will be used to treat Maine and New Hampshire roads come winter), cable ships (ships that help lay and maintain the transatlantic cable), coal barges, and of course, the sturdy tug boats, guiding the big ships through the treacherous channel. Cormorants, black sea birds with necks crooked like cranes, follow the ships in and out and can often be seen basking on the buoys. How long the bridge is up depends on the size of the ship going through, or on how many craft are making their way up or downstream. If it's a big tanker, or a flotilla of sailboats, be prepared for a wait. It's not uncommon for folks to shut off their cars and walk up to the bridge to watch the boats pass by. If you have to wait, you might as well enjoy the view!

Fishing, lobstering, and shipbuilding are still a key part of Kittery's economy and there are many places to see them taking place. For a look at shipbuilding then and now, visit the **Portsmouth Naval Shipyard.** The shipyard is not far from the Memorial Bridge (in fact, you can see it from the bridge). Route 1 North brings you across the Memorial Bridge into Maine. Just after you cross the bridge, follow Route 1 to the top of the hill and a stop sign. Go right at the stop sign onto Government Street. This leads you down to the first gate to the "Yard."

Despite its name, the Yard is located in Kittery, spanning five islands in the harbor. The Yard opened in 1806, as a builder of sailing ships. The *Ranger,* John Paul Jones's famous eighteen-gun sloop, was built here. Built in 1777, the *Ranger* was the first American "Man of War," and the first to fly the new American flag. The

Ranger was also the first American ship to receive a salute from a foreign nation—from the French at Quiberon Bay in 1778. During the Revolutionary War, with the daring John Paul Jones at the helm, the *Ranger* captured many prizes and played a pivotal role in the war at sea.

Commodore Isaac Hull, who led the legendary USS *Constitution* into battle during the War of 1812, was the first commandant of the Portsmouth Naval Shipyard. "Old Ironsides," as the *Constitution* was affectionately known, was once overhauled at the Yard. Civil War hero Admiral David Farragut (known for the phrase "Damn the torpedoes. Full speed ahead!") is buried here. The Yard is also home to "the Castle," once a prison for the Navy's most incorrigible inmates. At its construction in 1908, it was the largest poured-concrete building in the world. Several movies were later filmed here (among them *The Last Detail* with a very young Jack Nicholson). Even four-legged animal heroes are recognized at the Yard. There is a special animal cemetery where the likes of Old Tom, a valiant cavalry horse who served in the Spanish-American War, and other brave "warriors" are buried.

The Yard's motto is "Sails to Atoms," and its history encompasses mechanized ships and submarines. During World War II, the Portsmouth Naval Shipyard built more than half the submarine fleet and set records in sub production, turning out thirty-two subs in 1944 alone. Several famous subs are associated with the Yard. The *L8*, the country's first real submarine, was launched here in 1917. In the 1930s, the submarine *Squalus* made headlines when it foundered and sank just off the Isles of Shoals. Most of the crew were rescued successfully thanks to use of an experimental underwater chamber. The *Squalus* was brought up, towed to the Yard, rebuilt, and renamed the *Sailfish*. She went on to serve in World War II. (The *Squalus* is the subject of the 1999 bestseller *The Terrible Hours* by Peter Maas.) In 1953, the *Albacore* was built. At the time, there were none like her anywhere in the world. Her unique hydrodynamic shape was designed by Yard engineers, making her extremely fast, quiet, and highly maneuverable. The *Albacore* was the most advanced sub of its day and a forerunner of today's nuclear fleet. The actual *Albacore* is now permanently berthed in Portsmouth, N.H., off Market Street. It is open to the public for tours. Call (603) 436-3680 for more information.

Today, nuclear submarines are repaired at the Yard. You can learn more about these submarines and the Yard's rich history by visiting the **Portsmouth Naval Shipyard Museum.** Here there are artifacts from famous battleships, from World War II, the *Squalus, Albacore,* and many other submarines. You can also take a tour of the Yard's "Heritage Trail," which includes the animal cemetery and more than fifty buildings on the National Register of Historic Places. Call (207) 438-1000 for hours and more information about arranging a tour. A phone call is necessary, as tours are usually by appointment and a pass is required to access the Yard. Because the Yard is still active, it is subject to all the security requirements of any other military or government installation and restrictions do apply. There may be times when access is not allowed, so again, call ahead.

Fishing and lobstering are done all along the Kittery/Kittery Point coastline, but one of the best places to see working boats is from **Fort McClary State Park,** on Route 103 in Kittery Point. You can pick up Route 103 by continuing north on Government Street to the junction of 103. Turn right, and head east toward Kittery Point and the forts.

Fort McClary was built in 1846 and named for Andrew McClary, who died at the battle of Bunker Hill. A striking hexagonal blockhouse sits atop the hillside, offering panoramic views of the Piscataqua River, the harbor, two lighthouses, and the Isles of Shoals, a cluster of nine rocky islands several miles off the coast. The blockhouse is a wooden fort with a projecting second story. You can still see the openings in the walls where defenders would have manned their guns. Fishermen and lobstermen work these waters daily and can be seen checking and hauling traps. Fort McClary is also a wonderful place for exploring and picnicking. The multi-story blockhouse is open to the public, as are several other outbuildings. A fascinating stone tunnel leads from the fort to the shore; it tends to be damp, but is wonderfully eerie. Kids will enjoy creating a little history of their own, while adults can relax and revel in the views. Fort McClary is fully accessible from Memorial Day to Labor Day. In the fall, full facilities are typically available on weekends through to Columbus Day. In winter, you can visit the park, but parking is outside the gate and there are no facilities. The admission fee during the summer season is a nominal donation.

Just beyond Fort McClary, as you continue east on Route 103, is **Cap'n Simeon's Galley** and the **Frisbee General Store,** both located on the right side of Route 103. Cap'n Simeon's is right on a lobster pier. Feel free to walk down and see the boats come in. If you are lucky enough to be seated by the window in the restaurant, enjoy the boats and a spectacular harbor view while you dine. Cap'n Simeon's is a family-friendly restaurant offering all manner of seafood at reasonable prices. It is a great place to get your first taste of Maine lobster! Kids menu choices are available.

The neighboring **Frisbee General Store** was opened by the Frisbee family in 1828, and is still run by subsequent generations. It is the oldest family-owned general store in North America. The store first opened its doors when John Quincy Adams was in the White House. Today, the sixth generation of Frisbees sell the groceries. Although the store carries premium brands such as Pepperidge Farm, Oakhurst, and Green Mountain, the atmosphere is definitely from an earlier time. Folks still gather around the pot-bellied stove, and the cash register dates from the 1890s. The ceiling is tin, installed in 1912, and the display cases, filled with candy and other goods, are oak and glass. An old wooden sign from the 1840s hangs over the produce corner: TOBACCO, CIGARS, DRY GOODS. CONFECTIONERY, PATENT MEDICINE, it proclaims. Lollipops are still a penny, while other types of candy range from 2 to 5 cents. The Frisbee store still stocks Mary Janes and Walnettos. The pier where Cap'n Simeon's now sits was also once part of the Frisbee enterprise.

Frisbee's specializes in local products: baked goods, jams, jellies, eggs, produce, and even local wine. They cut their own beef and steaks and grind their own hamburg. The baked goods are made by the family, as are the barbecued chicken and ribs and the items in the deli. For a true taste of old-time Maine (with just a dash of newer premium foods), visit Frisbee General Store, which is open year-round.

About a mile down the road, Route 103 splits to the left, and Chauncey Creek Road continues to the right. Follow Chauncey Creek Road to the Gerrish Island bridge and the turn for **Fort Foster,** a town park. Fort Foster is an 88-acre mix of meadows, forest, and beaches. It is the site of a real fort, and kids will enjoy clambering about the ramparts and outbuildings and discovering the gun turrets and towers located throughout the park. Fort Foster was built in 1872 to protect the coastline. It continued to be a defensive site even through World War II.

On one side of the park is a **sandy beach,** which is usually not crowded. Depending on the weather, surf generally is pretty gentle here, so the beach is good for swimming and wading. Although park rangers make the rounds, no lifeguard is on duty at the park, so parents need to be present. The park is also a popular base for sea kayakers.

Even in summer, the Atlantic Ocean is cold. Temperatures in June and July average in the fifties, and by August, the water may have warmed up to the low sixties. Native Mainers do swim from June on, but to those from warmer climates, the "refreshing" briskness of the waters of Maine may come as a shock! (Amazingly, children never seem to mind the chillier water. It is very common to see even toddlers paddling about in the surf for hours.)

Above the sandy beach is a **560-foot wooden pier,** which is worth the walk. At the end of the pier, a spacious area with benches is a perfect spot to sit and enjoy the view. This is a great place for taking photographs, fishing, or relaxing. From here, you can see the bright cluster of sailboats at the Isles of Shoals, six miles out, two lighthouses, and all the craft moving up and down the river. Next to the pier, note the old Coast Guard station, and the remains of the bridge that once led to it.

Children tidepooling at Fort Foster. The remains of the fort and the playground are in the background.

Fort Foster has an **extensive network of paths,** which lead along the beach, through the woods and marsh, or through the meadows. Wildlife is abundant, ranging from ducks, deer, foxes, rabbits, and turkeys, to seals who occasionally sun themselves along the rocky shore (see sidebar on wildlife, page 123). If you visit around Columbus Day, you also may be treated to the sight of hundreds of monarch butterflies feeding on the many bushes as they get ready to migrate to Mexico.

The other side of the park is rockier and great for **tidepooling,** seashell collecting, or watching the surf. Never been tidepooling? Tidepooling is exploring those shallow, rocky pools of water left by the retreating tide. Many such pools are teeming with marine life, and hunting for sea stars, sea urchins, mussels, snails, and other residents of tidepools is a great way to learn about these mysterious ocean creatures. Many bookstores offer field guides; Golden Books puts out an excellent full-color guide suitable for kids and adults alike. You might want to bring a mesh scoop for picking up tidepool animals, and an inexpensive magnifying glass for taking a closer look. Remember, these are all living animals, so handle with care and return them to where you found them.

Fort Foster has picnic tables, grills, a playground, and restrooms. You can easily spend a few hours or a day at this lovely coastal spot. The season is similar to Fort McClary, with full access and facilities from Memorial Day to Labor Day and weekends offering full facilities through Columbus Day. The park may be visited during the winter, but parking is outside the gate and no facilities are available. Admission is charged during the summer season.

Follow the access road from Fort Foster back to the stop sign. At the stop sign, go right onto Chauncy Creek Road to Seapoint Road, which leads to **Seapoint Beach.** Seapoint is a wild beach and part of the Rachel Carson Wildlife Reserve. There are no facilities of any kind, but it is a great place for exploring, tidepooling, or just racing along the sand. There are usually no crowds. You can swim or wade, but since there are no lifeguards, caution is advised. A visit to a beach like Seapoint offers a unique taste of what beaches were like long ago: just wind, waves, sand, and rock. Breathe the salt air. Listen to the gulls. Hear the sounds of the sea.

Picnicking is allowed at Seapoint, but it will be a blanket picnic on the sand or rocks; there are no tables. Parking is only for Kittery residents, so you will need to find a place to leave your car and hike or bike to the beach. About a quarter mile before you reach the beach, there is a very small parking area on your right. In the summer months, these slots fill up quickly, so plan to arrive early or come later in the day. A second lot closer to the beach is only for Kittery Point residents and you will be ticketed if you park there.

Both Fort Foster and Seapoint Beach are great for kite flying, since they get the gusty east wind. It is not uncommon to see some spectacular kites aloft at either place.

Looping back toward Kittery proper on Route 103, you will see signs for U.S. Route 1. Route 1 in Kittery is home to more than 125 **outlet stores** and the **Kittery Trading Post.** You may not get to visit every outlet store, but the Kittery Trading Post is worth a stop.

In 1938, the Trading Post opened its doors as a small retailer of bows, firearms, and hunting goods. Local hunters brought deerskins and other pelts to trade. Over time, the store grew and grew, and with each expansion, a more diverse selection of outdoor merchandise was offered. Today, the Kittery Trading Post rivals L. L. Bean in scope. Everything for outdoor wear and sporting goods is available, from kayaks to canoes, rods and reels, boots and bows. Gift items such as jewelry, books, and compact disks are also sold. Even if you are not looking to buy, the Trading Post is worth a visit for the outstanding taxidermy displays. A giant moose, a black bear stretched to its full height, magnificent deer, and many other animals tower above shoppers or crouch among the merchandise.

If you like to shop, the **outlet malls** along Route 1 offer a huge selection of stores, including many specializing in children's clothing, books, and toys. Other goods include china, sunglasses, silverware, clothes, leather goods, linens, jewelry, kitchenware, furniture, luggage, sporting goods, audio disks and videotapes, tools, candles, crystal, collectibles, and craft items. There are numerous family-style and fast-food restaurants along the outlet corridor. Rain or shine, the outlets draw a crowd in the summer months. Good buys can be found, but be prepared for slow-moving traffic and possibly having to hunt for a parking place. For more information, call 1-888-KITTERY or visit **www.thekitteryoutlets.com**.

◢ Lobster Lore

Visitors to Maine typically think of lobsters as steamed and served with melted butter. But to Mainers, lobsters are an important marine animal that they must harvest from the sea. Although most lobstering is done during the milder months, some lobstermen run their boats year-round, braving rain, wind, snow, and the treacherous Atlantic to bring in this valuable catch. Most lobstermen know quite a bit about this hardy animal. Here are some facts:

The American lobster is common to the Northeast. Lobsters normally have two claws, one for tearing their food and one for holding or crushing. It is not unusual to find lobsters with only one claw, as they may lose a claw in a fight with other lobsters or when fleeing some danger. The missing claw eventually can grow back.

A lobster does not see images the way we do. The lobster uses sensory bristles (similar to whiskers) that cover its entire body to touch, taste, and help it find its way around the ocean floor. For example, the bristles on the lobster's antennae sense chemicals in the water. The shorter bristles on the inside of its walking legs and on some of its mouth parts allow the lobster to taste potential food.

Lobsters usually walk along the ocean bottom, but can move through the water if they have to. If danger threatens, a lobster will flap its tail to propel itself back through the water, all the while clicking its claws at its attacker.

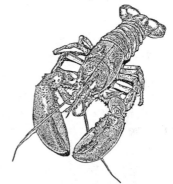

American lobster.

What do lobsters eat? A wide variety of fish and invertebrates, including other lobsters! When full grown, a lobster may reach a length of more than 3 feet and weigh more than 45 pounds.

Typically, lobsters are greenish-black in color, but blue, red, and albino specimens have been found. (The red lobsters typically pictured on restaurant signs and menus have been cooked; lobsters turn red when cooked.)

Many of these crafty crustaceans become adept at avoiding traps, and once they reach maturity (having survived fish that would prey on young lobsters), they may live to a ripe old age. In the wild, lobsters can live to be forty years old, or older. Lobstermen will leave an older female lobster, knowing that she is more valuable for the young she will produce than as a catch.

◢ Tidepool Tips

Meet a few of the creatures you are likely to find in our local tidepools:

The **northern moon snail** could easily be called "Big Foot." Its large foot is a handy tool for catching clams and mollusks. When it finds dinner, the moon snail pins the animal with its big foot, then drills through the shell with its toothed tongue to get to the food inside.

Northern moon snail.

Moon snails get their name from their large, round, bluish-white shells. The snail seems too big for its shell, but can hide completely inside if frightened.

Do you see a "walking pincushion?" If so, you've found a **sea urchin.** The urchin's hard, spiny shell protects its soft body. The animal's mouth is on the underside of its body, so it eats as it crawls along, scraping algae off rocks with sharp, little teeth. Sea urchins are also masters of disguise, using their tiny tube feet to cover themselves with seaweed and small rocks for camouflage.

What story does the **sand dollar** tell? Legend has it that the sand dollar shows the birth and resurrection of Christ. An Easter Lily, the Star of Bethlehem, a Christmas poinsettia, and a bell are all outlined on the animal's shell. The Easter Lily and poinsettia markings are really rows of tube feet, which allow the

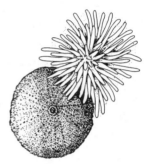

Sea Urchin with sea anemone.

animal to move and burrow in the sand. Sand dollars eat tiny plants and animals. They range in color from dark brown to red, and are covered with a felt-like coating of spines.

Sand dollar.

You may find several types of **sea stars** in tidepools on the Maine coast. Two of them are the blood star and the common sea star. Blood stars can be purple, yellow, red, orange, or even flesh-colored. They feed almost exclusively on sponges, and are common to tidepools and rocky shallows. The skin of a blood star is grainy to the touch, with more equal-sized spines. Blood stars generally grow about 2 inches across.

The common sea star, as its name suggests, is fairly abundant, and also very colorful. It can be found in shades of olive, brown, yellow, orange, red, and purple. The young ones are almost white. The tube feet of these sea stars are

Blood star.

in four rows, while all other species have two rows of feet. Common sea stars can grow up to 16 inches across, and are found from Labrador to Cape Cod in tidepools, on jetties and pilings, or on sand and stone beaches.

Common sea star.

🖋 *Can You Dig for Clams?*

Unfortunately, there is not a clear answer. You will need to ask at the local town hall in the town where you wish to dig. There are state requirements, but local rules may be stricter. Digging for clams, or harvesting of other shellfish, even for personal use, is often restricted to residents of Maine. To be considered a resident, you must have lived in Maine for at least six months prior to requesting a license; you must be registered to vote in Maine; and you must hold a Maine driver's license. You should also be aware that different licenses are required for different types of harvesting. A license for lobstering doesn't cover shellfish, a shellfish license doesn't cover mussels. A separate permit is required for harvesting seaweed or worms. If you have moved to Maine recently, and fit the resident criteria, then you should check with your town hall about the permits required. In addition to state licenses, many communities have local requirements that must also be met. Most town offices will have a copy of the state's *Marine Fishery Laws and Regulations,* which clearly outlines all permit requirements.

Kittery Highlights at a Glance

- Memorial Bridge on Route 1 in Kittery
- Portsmouth Naval Shipyard and Museum off Route 1 in Kittery: (207) 438-1000
- Fort McClary State Park on Route 103 in Kittery Point
- Cap'n Simeon's Galley on Route 103 in Kittery Point: (207) 439-3655
- Frisbee General Store on Route 103 in Kittery Point: (207) 439-0014

- Fort Foster off Route 103 in Kittery Point: (207) 439-2182
- Seapoint Beach off Route 103 in Kittery Point
- Kittery Trading Post on Route 1 in Kittery: (207) 439-2700
- Outlet Malls on Route 1 in Kittery: 1-888-KITTERY
- Maine Tourism Association: (207) 439-1319

Come enjoy some of the state's most popular family beaches, plus a landmark saltwater taffy shop, old-time amusement park, York's Wild Kingdom, and historic Nubble Light. Take a stroll through Old York, enjoy one of the Ghostly Tours, and walk the renowned Marginal Way. Other activities include boat cruises, the Center for Wildlife, hiking, picnicking, the Wiggly Bridge, trolley rides, and the wild beauty of Mount Agamenticus.

The Yorks

Route 1 leads you to some of the best family beaches in the state, and three of the loveliest communities: **York Village, York Harbor, and York Beach.**

Turn off Route 1 onto Route 1A heading east and you will soon enter **York Village.** York Village takes you back in time, as the community boasts a remarkable collection of historic homes, churches, and cemeteries. York is the first chartered city in America, dating from 1641. This well-preserved section of the downtown is called **Old York** and most of the buildings here date back to the 1700s. Many of them are still owned by descendants of the original builders. Seven of them are open to the public, and they are within walking distance of each other in York Village. The best place to start is the Jeffords Tavern Visitors Center, which is a right turn off Route 1A onto Lindsay Road, directly across from the First Parish Church, one of York's signature landmarks. Here you can obtain information about the seven sites and a map. The tavern is known for its old-fashioned tap room and bar, "retiring rooms" for the ladies, and welcoming common room. A tavern such as this was a godsend for colonial travelers seeking food, drink, and lodging. From here, walk to the First Parish Church and Meeting House, dating from 1747 and still an active parish today. Stroll the Village Green

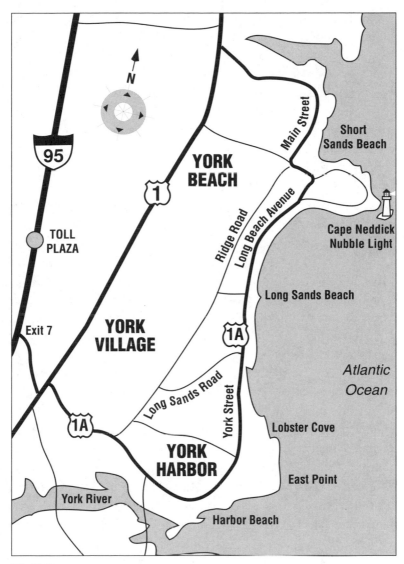

The Yorks

The York area is known for its great family beaches, famous Nubble Light, and historic Old York, where you can step back in time to sample life in colonial days. *Map by Denise Brown of Ad-Cetera Graphics.*

where men from York have mustered for war since 1753. See the tablet that honors those who went to fight at Lexington and Concord. Experience the dungeons and cells of the Old Gaol Museum, and have your photos taken in the stocks. Take your place with colonial pupils and learn your lessons at the schoolhouse. Look smart, for the schoolmaster is strict! Near the water, stop by the John Hancock Warehouse and Wharf. This working pier was once owned by this signer of the Declaration of Independence. Several other historic homes in this area are also open and furnished to their appropriate periods. Throughout your visit to Old York, you will hear stories of long ago and watch costumed role players re-enact colonial life as you visit each building.

Old York offers many **activities for all ages.** Some highlights include the Jail Break, a program that features a tour of the Old Gaol and its tales of mysterious escapes and notorious criminals. The tour is conducted by lantern light and costumed interpreters lead the way. Other offerings include lessons in hearth cooking, whereby visitors actually make a colonial dessert; basket weaving (make a candy basket), or spending an afternoon at the Old Schoolhouse, writing with a quill pen, making a copy book, and rolling hoops, a popular game with children of yesteryear. For a complete immersion in the past, check out Colonial Kids Camp, which lets children spend a week in the eighteenth century. Past activities have included making marbleized paper, spinning, weaving, dipping candles, dressing in colonial costume, and cooking a meal on the hearth. For more information on the camp, and all the Old York Activities, call (207) 363-4974 or visit **www.oldyork.org**. Many activities, such as the Jail Break, do require a reservation, so plan to call ahead.

The homes and historic sites that comprise Old York are open mid-May to mid-October, and an admission is charged. All seven sites are walkable, but little legs might find some of the distances tiring. The longest distance is to the Perkins House, which is three-quarters of a mile from Jeffords Tavern. The John Hancock Warehouse and George Marshall Store are side by side and are about a half mile from the tavern. The other sites are clustered more closely together around the green. If your children are too young to walk, the more distant sites can be visited by car.

While Old York is a wonderful stop in summer, great family celebrations occur in fall and at Christmas. On a Saturday in mid-October, the historic village wakes to the sound of fife and drums as the York Militia, a colonial troop, marches into town. The town crier, in full period costume, mounts the steps of the First Parish Church and proclaims that the harvest is in and the celebration should begin. The reverend gives thanks and **Harvestfest** is underway. You will find a myriad of wonderful buys at the hundreds of craft booths lining the church grounds and side streets. Under the big dining tent, every kind of food is served, from lobster and chowder to homemade pies, burgers, sausages, chili, and much more. Throughout the day, musical acts perform, ranging from Irish stepdancers to folk singers. The militia encamps across the street and periodically strikes a tune or fires off their cannons. Hayrides take visitors through the village, which is especially picturesque with the fall foliage. Early to mid-October is prime foliage season in southern Maine, so you can expect to see oaks, maples, and other hardwoods ablaze with a mix of reds and golds.

One of the dining highlights is the Ox-Roast and Bean-Hole Baked Beans. In colonial fashion, an ox is roasted overnight in an outside pit on the church grounds. Beans bake in another pit. All day long, the tempting smell wafts through the crisp fall air, and locals and visitors alike line up to partake of this old-fashioned New England tradition. For dates and information on this year's Harvestfest weekend, call the York Chamber of Commerce at (207) 363-4422, or visit **www.gatewaytomaine.org**. There is no admission to the festival itself.

Christmastime also brings a special flavor to the Village with the **Festival of Lights** celebration. Fairs, caroling, Santa Claus, and the annual Holiday Parade, plus numerous church suppers mark the start of the holiday season in York. For more information on this year's festival, contact the chamber.

Another great way to see the Village is by night as part of the **Ghostly Tours.** Ghostly Tours depart from the Graveyard Art store, which is on your left as you head east down the main street (Route 1A). While waiting for the tour to start, be sure to browse the store's unique collection of ghoulish and mystical items, including their signature shirts, featuring gravestone rubbings from local and regional graves.

The tour leader appears dressed as the Grim Reaper and carrying a lantern. The tour weaves through the downtown with numerous stops as the Reaper shares ghost stories, local legends, and folklore. The highlight of the tour is a visit to the Old Burying Ground, which bears the legendary gravestone of a witch. The grave of Mary Nason is partially covered by a large stone block, which is said to help keep the witch in place. (In truth, her husband placed the stone to keep pigs and cattle away.) For more information on Ghostly Tours, or to make a reservation (strongly suggested), call (207) 363-0000. The Graveyard Art store is easily found. As you come into York Village on Route 1A east, continue past the monument on into the center of town. The store is on your left.

Continuing along Route 1A, you will next come to **York Harbor.** York Harbor is one of the prettiest little harbors in Maine, with boats riding at anchor, classic white homes with turrets and gables, and several famed inns lining the shore. To truly experience some of Maine's famous heritage, consider a day on the ocean, either fishing or whale-watching. You can set sail for either one from York Harbor, as both fishing charters and whale-watches run from here. One of the more extensive operations is **Bigger 'n Better Sportfishing.** Call (207) 363-7406 or visit **www.biggernbetter.com.** For a complete list of boat charters, contact the York Chamber of Commerce.

Most sportfishing boats run from Memorial Day to Labor Day. Some charters will go out in good weather in late spring or early fall—anywhere from late April to early November—but waters can be rougher then. If you are vacationing in spring or fall, your best bet is to call the local chamber, or one of the charters mentioned in this book, to see if any fishing trips are available.

No one can visit Maine without enjoying a clambake and one of the premier clambake preparers is **Foster's Downeast Clambake** here in York Harbor, off Route 1A. Foster's has been hosting clambakes since 1951. Their skill has taken them around the world, and has included creating a clambake on the White House lawn, and on another occasion, presenting a celebratory dinner for 4,600 troops returning from the Gulf War. Foster's will prepare a clambake at their rustic pavilion, or bring the clambake to your location of choice. Every clambake features these traditional ingredients: chowder (theirs has won awards), freshly dug clams and mussels, Maine lobster, corn on the cob, Red Bliss potatoes, and roasted onions. All are served with drawn butter and freshly baked rolls. (If you think your little ones might not be ready for a lobster, Foster's also has chicken or vegetarian selections and a kids' menu.) Dessert is usually blueberry crumb cake.

On a cool day, your clambake at Foster's will be inside by the roaring stone fireplace. On a nice day, dine outside in their shady pavilion. Clambakes at Foster's are a good time for all. In addition to great Maine food, they include sing-alongs and other live entertainment, shuffleboard, volleyball, basketball, and horseshoes. All in all, a great way to work up an appetite! Young and old alike may also find themselves wearing the unique Foster's "lobster hats." After all, it is tradition!

Foster's clambakes are all by reservation. At certain times, they may also require groups of ten or more. However, if your group is smaller, you can still enjoy a clambake by calling and being "partnered" with another clambake group. Foster's will let you know when they are serving other clambakes and your smaller party will be booked for one of those dates. Whatever the situation, they always strive to accommodate guests and make sure no one misses out on a chance at a Maine clambake. Foster's primarily serves clambakes from Memorial Day through mid-October, but occasionally does special bookings into November and December. Call (207) 363-3255 for more details.

A favorite hiking and photography spot is down by the **Wiggly**

Bridge—a slight detour off Route 1A at York Harbor onto Route 103 on your right. The Wiggly Bridge is a suspended footbridge over the York River that leads to the 16-acre **Stedman Woods Bird Sanctuary.** Children love to run back and forth over the bouncing bridge, and the woods are an interesting hike, but not too long a walk for shorter legs. Shore, marsh, and songbirds are sighted frequently. You might see egrets wading or plovers scurrying along the shore. Listen for the calls of black-capped chickadees, blue jays, and marsh sparrows. Best viewing times are early in the day or near twilight. The sanctuary is open year-round, and there is no admission.

Follow Route 103 back to Route 1A. Route 1A now curves along to York's famous beaches: **Long Sands** and **Short Sands.** You will come to Long Sands first, which is easily visible on your right-hand side as you head north. There is parking all along 2-mile Long Sands beach, but arrive early, as space fills up quickly, and bring plenty of quarters if you plan to spend the day. There is no fee to use the beach itself. A short stretch of pebbles separates the beach proper from the sidewalk, but once you cross those, it is all one

Long Sands Beach in York. *Photo by Marcia Peverly.*

long stretch of pure sand. Surf can get high here after a storm, but in general this is a safe, family beach with no sudden drop-offs or strong undertows, and lifeguards are present. (Please note that lifeguards and bathhouses are generally only available from Memorial Day to Labor Day. Please also see the special sidebar on storms on page 83.) Long Sands is great for body surfing, swimming, kite flying, and generally enjoying a perfect day at the beach. If you wish to spend more than a day, rows and rows of cottages stand across from the entire expanse. Contact the York Chamber or the Maine Tourism Association (207) 439-1319 for information on rentals.

Before getting to Short Sands, stop at one of the nation's most famous lighthouses, **Cape Neddick Light,** or as it is more popularly known, **Nubble Light.** Captain John Smith gave it its nickname because he said it stood on a "nubble" of land. It is said that Nubble Light is one of the most photographed lighthouses in the country. Built in 1879 on a small island off the coast of Cape Neddick, the gleaming white lighthouse sits on a small grassy slope next to a charming white cottage and red and white outbuildings. The Nubble is still a working lighthouse, although it is now fully auto-

Cape Neddick Light, also called Nubble Light, in Cape Neddick. *Photo by Marcia Peverly.*

mated. Today, it is owned by the Town of York and managed by the Friends of Nubble Light. Because the channel separating the island from the mainland is narrow, it is possible to get quite close to the Nubble, providing an outstanding opportunity for great pictures. In late November, crowds gather for the annual Lighting of the Nubble. The lighthouse and its accompanying buildings are outlined in lights, creating a spectacular vision against the night sky. Carols are sung, Santa appears, and cocoa is served to the faithful who brave the cold to witness this tradition. Nubble Light is accessed easily from Route 1A; simply follow the signs for the lighthouse and Nubble Road on your right.

Offshore from the Nubble is another famous lighthouse, **Boon Island Light,** the tallest lighthouse in Maine and New England at 133 feet. It is 6.5 miles from the Nubble, on a small, rocky, barren spit of land. This slim, brown tower has a darker reputation, as it was once the site of a horrific shipwreck and its gruesome aftermath. In December of 1710, the British ship *Nottingham Galley* wrecked on Boon Island. Survivors struggled to stay alive for three weeks, as storms continued to batter the island and their waves, combined with an extra high tide, threatened to engulf the entire rocky outcropping. There was no food nor water, and so the castaways resorted to cannibalism, eating those who died from the wreck and later of exposure. After this disaster, local fishermen began leaving barrels of provisions (a "boon") on the island in case of future wrecks. The British shipwreck, and its consequences, were immortalized in Kenneth Roberts's book *Boon Island.* The island is full of many other tales and any local book store will have at least one book with stories of Boon Island.

Upon leaving the Nubble, continue on Route 1A to **Short Sands.** Short Sands, also easily visible on your right, is an equally pleasing family beach, although smaller in size than Long Sands. There is extensive metered parking in the large lot next to the beach, and there is no fee to use the beach itself. Short Sands has a different character than Long Sands. Because the beach area is smaller and more bowl-shaped, surf can be higher here and there can be stronger currents. This is still a safe swimming beach, however, and lifeguards are present. Many rocky outcroppings at either end of the beach make for lots of places to tidepool and search for marine life. Younger children will also enjoy the playground set in the soft sand right near the beach. A sidewalk, benches, and a gazebo also line the beach, making this a great place to stroll and take in not only the surf but also some of York's grand old hotels on the opposite side.

Both beaches are available to the public year-round, but again, lifeguards and bathhouses are generally only available Memorial Day to Labor Day.

Just past Short Sands is a cluster of shops, arcades, and one of York Beach's most famous landmarks, **The Goldenrod,** a combination candy shop and restaurant. For more than one hundred years, the Goldenrod has been a mainstay of the beach area. Kids cluster around the window to watch real saltwater taffy being made. The taffy is stretched and twisted, then cut, compacted, and wrapped into "kisses." There are dozens of flavors and few folks leave York Beach without a box of taffy. The Goldenrod also serves fudge and other fine candies, makes their own ice cream, and has a real old-fashioned soda fountain. Visitors also enjoy dining in their rustic dining room (prices are reasonable for a family). If you want a taste of summer to send to a friend, ask the Goldenrod to ship a box of kisses—they send them all over the world. Call (207) 363-2621 for more information. The Goldenrod is generally open Memorial Day to Labor Day, but like many beach shops, may be open weekends to Columbus Day. If you are visiting after Labor Day, and think you will have a craving for kisses, call ahead!

Route 1A now loops back to Route 1. You will need to backtrack and head south briefly on Route 1 to reach **York's Wild Kingdom,** a zoo and amusement park that features creatures both familiar and exotic. The Kingdom allows visitors to get up close to elephants, kangaroos, tigers, zebras, lions, monkeys, and alpacas, to name just a few. It is also home to Maine's only white Bengal tiger. Little ones can feed the goats and ducks, and a wildlife theater offers daily shows.

The amusement park area offers rides that are for the most part on the gentler side: a smaller ferris wheel and roller coaster, merry go-round, go-carts, and an electric train. The wildest ride is the bumper cars. You can also play miniature golf. York's Wild Kingdom is open Memorial Day to mid-September; the amusement park closes on Labor Day. Admission is charged. You can buy tickets for both the park and the kingdom, or just one venue. Call (207) 363-4911 or 363-3883 for more information or visit **www.yorkzoo.com.**

For a glimpse of local wildlife, head north again on Route 1, then turn off onto Agamenticus Road on your left. Agamenticus Road leads you to the **Mount Agamenticus Wildlife Preserve and the Center for Wildlife.** The Center for Wildlife is a nonprofit organization that cares for injured wildlife of all kinds. On any given day, they may be working with hawks, owls, songbirds, raccoons, rabbits, squirrels, and many other animals. If you would like to visit the center, call first at (207) 361-1400. The Center accepts animals year-round, but since the mountain road is steep and winding, your best time to visit would be spring, summer, or fall, rather than winter. There is no admission, but donations are graciously accepted.

When you first crossed the Interstate 95 bridge into Maine, you may have noticed a small blue mountain off to the left. This is **Mount Agamenticus,** at 692 feet the highest point in York County, and also accessible from Agamenticus Road. Mount Agamenticus is said to be the home of the spirit gods of the local Abenaki Tribes, and indeed, where York now stands was once a Native American village called Agamenticus. At the top of Mount Agamenticus is a pile of stones recognizing St. Aspinquid, spiritual leader of the Abenakis and medicine man to many of the area tribes. His Native American name was believed to be Passaconaway, but when he converted to Christianity, he was called St. Aspinquid. When he died at the age of ninety-four in 1682, Indians came from hundreds of miles away to pay tribute to his memory, and legend has it that 6,723 wild animals were sacrificed here on the mountain to honor his memory. As was the Indian custom, his grave was covered with stones. Visitors are invited to add a stone to the pile in his honor.

Although the land around Mount Agamenticus is dotted with homes, much of the mountain area is still quite wild, and the 1,171-acre preserve is home to bear, deer, fisher, and many other species of wildlife. It is a great place to watch for hawks, eagles, and vultures soaring off into the blue. The area is heavily forested, but there are hiking trails and some of the best mountain biking in the state. Until recently, there were also stables for horseback riding and bike rentals, although those have not been open recently. There is talk they may resume, so you might call ahead and inquire.

If you plan to hike or bike, for safety reasons it is best to notify the Agamenticus lodge, or York Parks and Recreation, or bring your cell phone and have their numbers handy (note their phone numbers at the end of this paragraph). Although this is a wonderful preserve to explore, it is a wild area, and for any hikes in rough terrain, you should plan ahead. Bring water, snacks, and warm clothing—temperatures drop quickly late in the day and mornings are chilly. Many trails are fairly steep, as part of the mountain was once a ski area during the 1950s and 1960s. Mount Agamenticus offers spectacular views of the surrounding coastal region, good opportunities for photographing wildlife, and is home to a wide range of wildflowers. You may spot lady slippers and blue flags in May and June, and wild lily-of-the-valley in summer. For more information on the Mount Agamenticus Preserve, call York Parks and Recreation at (207) 363-1040, or the lodge at (207) 361-1102. This preserve is a great hike for older children, say age seven and up. Younger children may find the trails too long or steep. The preserve is accessible seven days a week. There is no official season dates for the preserve, but the safest hiking times for those not very familiar with the terrain are spring, summer, and fall.

Ogunquit

Take Agamenticus Road back to Route 1 and turn left to continue north to **Ogunquit** (pronounced O-gun-quit), whose name means "beautiful place by the sea." Upon entering Ogunquit, your first

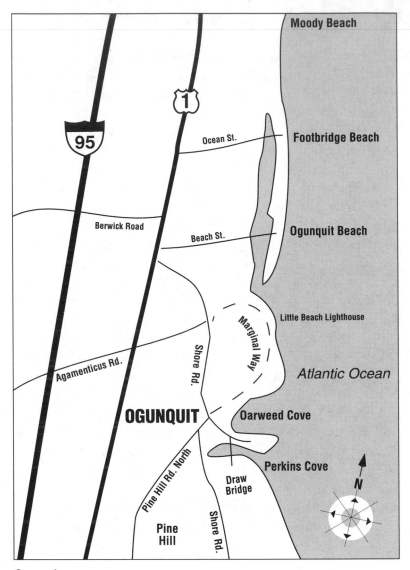

Moody Beach

95

1

Ocean St.

Footbridge Beach

Berwick Road

Beach St.

Ogunquit Beach

Marginal Way

Little Beach Lighthouse

Shore Rd.

Agamenticus Rd.

Atlantic Ocean

OGUNQUIT

Oarweed Cove

Pine Hill Rd. North

Draw Bridge

Perkins Cove

N

Pine Hill

Shore Rd.

Ogunquit

Ogunquit is one of the prettiest towns in southern Maine. Be sure to walk the Marginal Way and visit Perkins Cove, or maybe take a cruise on one of its many charter boats.

Map by Denise Brown of Ad-Cetera Graphics.

stop should be the **Ogunquit Chamber of Commerce,** on Route 1. The Chamber provides a beautiful Ogunquit booklet illustrating trolley routes and stops, parking areas, attractions, and public restrooms. This will make your visit much easier and more pleasant.

One of the easiest and most fun ways to get around Ogunquit is by **trolley.** The trolleys run frequently and efficiently, transporting you from parking areas around the town to Perkins Cove, beaches, and downtown shopping. All the trolleys are marked with the route they serve, and only a small fee is charged. It is an old-fashioned form of transportation that has regained popularity. The bell clangs and off you go, whirring down the town streets. People wave and it is fun riding in the open air.

Parking is fairly plentiful and there are lots allowing all-day parking, two-hour parking, and parking by the hour.

No visit to Ogunquit is complete without a stop at **Perkins Cove,** one of the most picturesque coves in Maine, and the **Marginal Way,** an ocean walk with spectacular views. If you choose not to take the trolley, then from Route 1, take Shore Road on your right down to the cove. In a state with many beautiful inlets, Perkins Cove still ranks as one of the loveliest. Small, cottage-style shops and eateries cluster around the cove, which is dotted with fishing boats. A small draw-footbridge goes up to let the boats pass in and out of the cove; this is the only bridge of its kind in New England. It is the same as the traditional drawbridge for cars, although downsized for foot traffic only. There is no more pleasant pastime than to get an ice cream or crabmeat roll, take a seat on a bench, and watch life in the cove. Here is the tuna catch being brought in (great 200-pound fish!), the passing of all manner of boats, the seabirds strutting along the docks or fluttering above the craft pestering for their fish, and the cool sea breeze washing over all.

Whale watching, deep-sea fishing and **lobstering cruises** all sail out of Perkins Cove. For a great day of whale watching, try the *Deborah Ann.* The *Deborah Ann* is a relatively small boat (running 40 feet), offering a more personal whale-watching experience than some of the larger cruise boats, which can get crowded. From her mooring at Perkins Cove, she sails to both the northern and southern parts of Jefferies Ledge, a prime whale-watching location. During the four-and-one-half hour cruise, watchers frequently see Atlantic white-sided dolphins, basking sharks, ocean sunfish, and finback, minke, and humpback whales.

So successful has the *Deborah Ann* been on her journeys that the crew guarantees sightings of dolphins, humpbacks, finbacks, and minke whales, with other rarer whales possible. If weather or movement of the whales prohibits sightings, the *Deborah Ann* extends a free pass with no expiration date. This is good for another trip, or one-half your money back.

For a cruise on the *Deborah Ann,* or any boat, dress warmly. Temperatures run 10 to 15 degrees cooler on the ocean. You also should bring sunscreen and your camera—don't miss a chance to photograph some incredible marine animals. Many cruises, including the *Deborah Ann,* do not have refreshment services on board. Bring your own snacks and beverages or call ahead to see what is offered. For more about the *Deborah Ann,* call (207) 361-9501. The *Deborah Ann* sails May to October; other boat schedules may vary.

Several deep-sea fishing boats also run out of Perkins Cove, including the *Bunny Clark* and the *Ugly Anne.* For more information on the *Ugly Anne,* call (207) 646-7202 or visit **www.uglyanne.com**. The *Bunny Clark* stands out a bit from other cruises because of its captain, Tim Tower. Tim is a native of Ogunquit and has been a commercial fisherman most of his life. He also holds a biology/chemistry degree and has worked as a marine biologist for the National Marine Fisheries Service and the Woods Hole Oceanographic Institute. For an exceptionally educational cruise, try the *Bunny Clark.* Call (207) 646-2214 for more information.

Whatever cruise you choose, most offer full- or half-day trips, rods, and reels; some also include bait. For a complete list of deep-sea and other charters, call the Ogunquit Chamber at (207) 646-2939.

One popular boat is the *Finestkind,* which offers a wide array of cruises, from scenic expeditions to Nubble Light and other sights, to breakfast and cocktail cruises, and even a lobstering trip. The lobstering trip explains how lobstering is done, shows traps being hauled, and allows cruisers to meet lobsters "up close and personal" and learn lobster lore. It is a great way to learn more about this vital part of Maine's heritage and economy. Reservations are recommended for all cruises, and visitors can call (207) 646-5227 for more information, or visit www.finestkindcruises.com.

All of these cruises primarily sail Memorial Day through Labor Day, but some also offer weekend trips in the fall or late spring. If you are coming pre-season or in the fall, call the Chamber, or the individual numbers, to confirm sailing dates.

All that time on the water can work up an appetite! There are many sandwich shops in the Cove, as well as a few restaurants (more restaurants abound throughout Ogunquit, both elegant and casual). One of the more famous places to eat is **Barnacle Billy's** at Perkins Cove, which serves a fine selection of traditional Maine food. Barnacle Billy's is known for its wonderful atmosphere—eat outside on the deck, or dine in by the fireplace. Either way, it is worth the experience. Lobster, chowders, and steamers have been served here for more than forty years. There is no children's menu per se, but Barnacle Billy's offers traditional kids favorites such as hot dogs, hamburgers, and grilled cheese sandwiches. Prices are reasonable for a family. Call (207) 646-5575 or visit www.barnbilly.com for a complete menu selection. Barnacle Billy's is open April through October.

After dining, or any time, take a stroll along the famed **Marginal Way,** which starts at Perkins Cove and is clearly marked. The Way is a winding footpath that follows the cliffs above the sea for more than a mile. The walk is easy but the cliffs are fairly high, so little ones should be taken in hand. The path is lined with wild roses in many spots and there are benches here and there so you can stop and sit a spell. The views are spectacular any time of day, but twilight is an especially pleasing time. The colors of sea and sky begin to soften; the moon begins to rise, and the evening air is perfumed with the scent of roses.

The Marginal Way ends at **Ogunquit Beach,** 3.5 miles of beautiful, smooth sand. (If you drive, rather than walk the Way, head north on Route 1 past Shore Road, and take Beach Street on your right.) Although popular, Ogunquit is one of the quieter beaches. No concessions, cottages, or amusements are located directly on the beach, making it an experience of sun, sand, and surf. There are four adjacent parking areas, and you pay when you enter the lots. The main beach lot has restrooms and changing areas, as does the footbridge lot. The main section of beach and the footbridge section both have lifeguards.

Most of the time, the surf at these beaches is pleasant and easily swimmable. However, if there is a storm, even offshore, beware. Surf has easily broken over the Marginal Way and nearby **Bald Head Cliff,** causing damage to property and in some cases, loss of life. If storms or high seas are forecast, do not attempt this cliff walk and keep well away from the shore.

After a day in the sun, take in some evening entertainment at the **Ogunquit Playhouse,** located right on Route 1, just as you enter Ogunquit. (From the cove and Marginal Way area, simply take Shore Road back to Route 1.) The Ogunquit Playhouse has been showcasing talent from Hollywood and Broadway, as well as local actors, for more than seventy years. The broad, white building with its ten green and white flags is a regional landmark. The Playhouse is set back from Route 1 on a sweeping expanse of manicured lawns, entered by an evergreen-lined drive. Inside, autographed photos of famous actors line the theater lobby. The Playhouse opened in 1937, and continues to offer popular summer theater. Dramas, comedies, musicals—there is something for everyone, from old favorites to new classics. While smaller children would find the evening long, those ages ten and up should enjoy some of the traditional musicals. Visit **www.ogunquitplayhouse.org** for show and ticket information, or call (207) 646-5511. The Ogunquit Playhouse is only open in summer.

If you are journeying to southern Maine later in the season, come for the **Cappriccio Festival of Kites** on Ogunquit Beach in early

September. Hundreds of kites of every design take to the skies, catching the last of the late-summer breezes. For more information, and this year's date, call (207) 646-6170.

✠ Fish Facts

If you go deep-sea fishing, or pursue any type of fishing, keep these fun facts in mind.

How Fish Breathe

Even though fish live underwater, they still need oxygen to breathe. Nearly all fish rely on gills to take in the oxygen dissolved in the water. Water is taken in over the fish's mouth and passed over the gills, which absorb the oxygen. Some species of fish can also breathe through their skin, and a mysterious few have lungs that permit them to breathe much like we do.

Fin Facts

All fish have fins, although they may look very different on different types of fish. Fins give fish both movement and stability. They help ward off predators and stir up food. Sometimes their shape helps a fish blend in with its environment and hide from possible attackers. Try to find each type of fin on the different fish you might see. What might each kind be used for? Think about how various fish eat and swim.

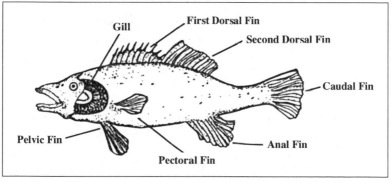

Fish fins.

If you go fishing, or go out on a deep-sea charter, take a moment to look for the gills on any fish you catch, or ask the captain to show them to you. Your captain can also talk about the uses of the fins on any fish you catch.

Why Are Fish in Schools?

When fishing, you may hear the captain or other fishermen around you say "Here comes a school of mackerel!" or some other species. A "school" of fish is just a big group of fish that swims together. Fish school for many reasons, but most have to do with avoiding predators. There is safety in numbers. Big groups lessen the odds of any one fish being eaten—with the safest fish being those in the middle of the group. Predators are also confused by so many fish swimming around at once.

◢ Tides

Life along the Maine coast is greatly influenced by the changing tides. Two high tides and two low tides occur every twenty-four hours, and the rivers, estuaries, and creeks connected to the ocean also follow this tidal rhythm. The changing of the tides is nature's way of refreshing and replenishing the coastal environment, and all the wildlife and plant life found there are adapted to this timeless ebb and flow.

When the tide goes out, it exposes an expanse of sand. Frequently, shallow pools of water are also left behind—called tidepools. The dense, wet sand is home to lots of food. Worms and clams live beneath its cool dampness and soon the area is alive with sea birds such as gulls, terns, plovers, and kittiwakes, who come to claim this bounty. Using beaks and claws, they extricate their prey from the wet sand. Humans also seek this food, digging for the succulent clams and harvesting the worms for fishing bait.

The tidepools are another source of food for seabirds and other wildlife. These pools of seaweed-covered rock teem with snails and mussels, sea stars, and occasionally even tiny lobsters or shrimp. Along tidal rivers, it is not unusual to see raccoons dipping into tidepools and feasting on the mussels or snails left behind.

When the tide comes in, the cooling water once again shelters and replenishes the animals in the tidepools. They can survive exposure to the warmth of the sun and the drying air for a certain period of time, but eventually need the protection of the ocean to survive. The daily return of the tide also ensures that the population of worms, clams, and tidepool animals continues to survive and grow, and is not over-harvested by people or wildlife.

Seaweed is also flung onto the beach and rocks by the incoming tide (and by waves during storms). In the past, farmers harvested the seaweed and put it on their fields, where it acted as a rich fertilizer. Today, only those with permits can remove the seaweed. Different types of seaweed are used not only as a natural fertilizer, but are also eaten cooked or raw and used in toothpaste, ice cream, and hair products as a smoothing and thickening agent.

The average tidal change in Maine takes two hours. This means that it takes about two hours for the tide to come in to its highest level, and it will take another two hours for the tide to go out to its lowest level. The range of high and low tide varies in response to the moon's cycles.

Beachgoers and beachcombers should pay attention to the tides. If you go to the beach and the tide is low, a larger expanse of beach will be available. However, be sure to note the high-tide mark, or the line between dry sand and damp. In a few hours, the tide will start to come in, gradually reclaiming part of the beach. Make sure your belongings are on dry ground, away from the incoming tide. Many folks camp right down near the water, often leaving their towels and coolers to go exploring. They are quite dismayed to return and find their items dampened by incoming waves, or worse, floating away!

Is high tide or low better for beachgoing? It's really a matter of taste. Many prefer low tide because they enjoy the larger sweep of beach. Children especially love having room to run, and enjoy the damp sand for building sand castles and other creations. They also like having more shallow water available for frolicking and paddling. Adults and more serious swimmers may prefer high tide because they don't have to wade out as far to swim. There also tends to be more surf for body surfing or boogie boarding on a high or incoming tide.

People of all ages should be aware of the incoming tide. The stronger surf and higher waves can knock little ones about, and the water is gradually getting deeper, so small children should stay close to shore. Even adults can be taken by surprise by an unexpectedly big wave sweeping in with the tide.

The tide can also come in faster in some areas than in others, depending on the geography of the area. Ask the locals about tide conditions and any idiosyncrasies before swimming in an unfamiliar area.

Beachcombers, obviously, prefer the beach at low tide because they have a greater area to explore. This is the time to find sea glass and shells, sand dollars and smooth stones, driftwood, and all the mysterious "gifts" swept in by the sea.

You can easily time your beach trip to the type of tide you want. The tides are given with every radio and TV weather report, shown on *The Weather Channel,* printed in the newspaper (see the Weather section), and tide charts are available at most any general store or beach shop, local Chamber of Commerce, or other tourist information center. Most town or state park beaches also have them posted.

The Yorks Highlights at a Glance

- Old York, on Route 1A, center of York Village: (207) 363-4974
- Harvestfest, held in York Village: (207) 363-4422
- Ghostly Tours, York Street in York Village: (207) 363-0000
- Bigger 'n Better Sportfishing, in York Harbor off Route 1A: (207) 363-7406
- Foster's Downeast Clambakes, in York Harbor, off Route 1A: (207) 363-3255
- Wiggly Bridge, in York Harbor, off Route 103
- Stedman Woods Bird Sanctuary, in York Harbor, off Route 103
- Long Sands, off Route 1A in York Beach
- Cape Neddick Light or Nubble Light, off Route 1A in York Beach
- Boon Island Light, off the coast of York Beach
- Short Sands, off Route 1A in York Beach
- The Goldenrod, off Route 1A in York Beach: (207) 363-2621
- York's Wild Kingdom, on route 1A in York Beach: (207) 363-4911 or 363-3883

- Mount Agamenticus Wildlife Preserve, off Route 1 on Agamenticus Road: (207) 363-1040
- Center for Wildlife off Route 1 on Agamenticus Road: (207) 361-1400
- York Chamber of Commerce, on Route 1, just off York Exit from I-95: (207) 363-4422

Ogunquit Highlights at a Glance

- Trolleys, run throughout Ogunquit
- Perkins Cove, off Shore Road from Route 1
- *Deborah Ann* at Perkins Cove: (207) 361-9501
- *Bunny Clark* at Perkins Cove: (207) 646-2214
- *Ugly Anne* at Perkins Cove: (207) 646-7202
- *Finestkind* at Perkins Cove: (207) 646-5227
- Barnacle Billy's at Perkins Cove: (207) 646-5575
- Marginal Way, starts at Perkins Cove
- Ogunquit Beach, Beach Street off Route 1
- Ogunquit Playhouse, on Route 1: (207) 646-5511
- Festival of Kites, at Ogunquit Beach: (207) 646-2939
- Ogunquit Chamber of Commerce: (207) 646-2939

Explore the 1,600-acre Laudholm Farm and enjoy nature activities such as bird-banding. Visit the area's famous beaches, the Wells Antique Auto Museum, Kennebunk Trolley Museum, and the Wedding Cake House. Look for Spouting Rock, Blowing Cave, and Walker's Point (you might glimpse a president!). Visit the marshes of the Rachel Carson Wildlife Refuge and go tidepooling, hiking, or picnicking. Stroll back in time at the Brick Store Museum and shop in the villages of Kennebunk and Kennebunkport.

From Ogunquit, continue north up Route 1 to **Wells,** a classic beachfront community (see map on page 37). Wells calls itself "the friendliest town in Maine," and indeed, the community atmosphere is very easygoing. Even the trolleys, which transport you from hotels to beaches, restaurants, shops, and even nearby Ogunquit, have cheery names. They are called "Katie," "Kelly," and "Karen." If you take the new Downeaster Train into Maine, Wells is one of the stops, and during the summer season, the trolleys meet the train.

Most of the activities in Wells are right off of Route 1, as opposed to following a "loop" as was suggested in Kittery or York. This can make for heavier traffic, since Route 1 is a main road, but it also means that everything is quite easy to find.

There is no question that one of Wells' major draws is its **miles of beaches.** Seven miles of wide, sandy beaches attract young and old alike. Swim, walk, run, play Frisbee or volleyball; this broad flat expanse is the perfect venue. The sand at Wells is fine and white and easy on hands and feet. After all that exertion, take time to sunbathe, read, build a sand castle, or just watch the waves roll in. All the beaches offer easy swimming and lifeguards are on duty. If smaller children have never been to the shore, Wells is a nice place to introduce them to life at the beach.

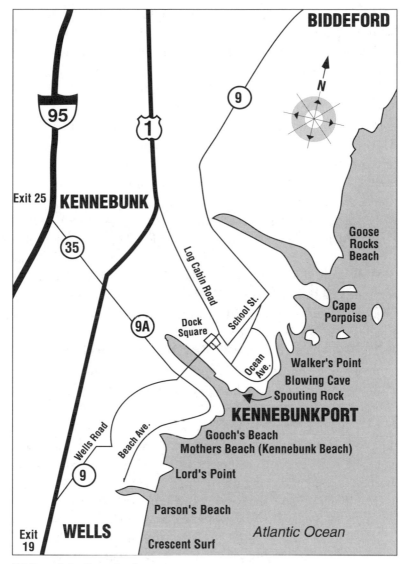

Wells and the Kennebunks

Wells offers miles of sandy beaches as well as great fishing. Be sure to visit the Wells Antique Auto Museum, the Museum of Lighthouse History and Lighthouse Depot, and Schoolhouse Division No. 9. The Kennebunk area is packed with things to do, from viewing natural wonders such as Spouting Rock, to glimpsing a president's home at Walker's point, or riding an old-time trolley at the Seashore Trolley Museum.

Map by Denise Brown of Ad-Cetera Graphics.

While access to the beaches is free, a nominal fee is charged for parking. A number of public parking areas are within easy reach of the beaches. If you are staying for an extended period, you can purchase a permit that offers a cheaper parking rate. (At this writing, the pass could be purchased at the parking area.)

Reaching any of the beaches is easy from Route 1. As you head north, turn right onto Bourne Avenue to access Ocean Avenue, which brings you to **Moody Beach.** To reach **Wells Beach,** continue on Ocean Avenue, which becomes Webhannet Avenue and then Atlantic Avenue, bringing you to Wells Beach. (You may also access Wells Beach directly from Route 1 by turning right onto Mile Road, which brings you down to Atlantic Avenue.) To visit Drakes Island Beach, take Drakes Island Road on your right from Route 1.

Wells is also home to a spectacular wild beach at the **Wells Reserve at Laudholm Farm.** The Reserve is just north of Drakes Island Road on Route 1. On your right, you will see Laudholm Road, and a sign for the Reserve.

The Wells National Estuarine Reserve was dedicated in 1986 with a mission to investigate coastal environments and enhance understanding of their ecology. The Reserve was created as a result of efforts by the Laudholm Trust, which was founded in 1982 to protect Laudholm Farm, where the Reserve is located. The Trust is a nonprofit organization that supports research, education, and management activities at the Reserve by working to increase public awareness and build community support.

The Wells Reserve spans 1,600 acres and includes a 7-mile trail system, which encompasses meadows, woodlands, marshes, and a wild beach. Wildlife is abundant and visitors may see deer, rabbits, raccoons, or porcupines in the woodland and meadow areas; egrets, herons, and bitterns at the marshes; and a range of shorebirds at the beach. It is not unusual to see seals in the cove just off the beach. The trails are open year-round. In the spring, the walk through the orchards is a treat when the apple trees are clouds of pink. Come early October, the forest foliage is at its peak, and the dense thickets of barberry blaze with red. In winter, the trails offer excellent cross-country skiing.

The historic original farmhouse and outbuildings still remain and have been put to good use. The farmhouse offers an amazing view in all directions, including not only the rolling expanse of field and forest, but also the ocean and Mount Agamenticus in the distance. Take a minute to rock on its wrap-around porch and enjoy this unbelievable panorama. Inside the farmhouse are exhibits on coastal ecology and a small gift shop. Other buildings now feature a library, research centers, offices, and auditorium. One of these, the **Maine Coastal Ecology Center,** includes research facilities, a teaching laboratory, and exhibits.

Laudholm Farm and the Wells Reserve offer a full slate of educational programs for children and families from spring through fall. Programs are hands-on and may include bird-banding, night walks, introductions to marine life, and other fascinating nature-based activities. Special half-day and full-day kids' camps provide lots of hands-on crafts, experiments, and explorations. For this year's schedule, or more information, call (207) 646-1555 or visit **www.wells reserve.org**.

Hiking in the reserve is easy. The trail guides and signage note the length of each trail, so it is appropriate to determine which trail is an appropriate walk for your children. Restroom facilities are available at the trailhead by the farm, but not once you are out on the trails or at the beach. There are picnic tables at the farm, but no refreshments are sold save for a soda machine at the restrooms. There is a fee for parking in the summer, but the trail system and exhibits are free. Any programs also charge a small fee. In general, the Reserve is accessible year-round, either for hiking spring through fall, or cross-country skiing come winter. Even in the off-season, the restrooms are typically open on weekends. The farmhouse visitors' center is open spring through fall.

Just up the road from the Wells Reserve is the **Rachel Carson National Wildlife Refuge.** Turn right off Route 1 North onto Route 9 and look for a sign for the Rachel Carson Refuge on the

The still beauty of the Rachel Carson Wildlife Refuge.

right. The Rachel Carson Refuge system actually encompasses ten different sites from Kittery to Cape Elizabeth, Maine. All of the sites are designed to protect coastal marshes for waterfowl and other migratory birds.

Rachel Carson was a world-famous marine biologist, author, and conservationist. Her signature work, *Silent Spring* (1962), linked the unrestrained use of chemical pesticides to severe biological consequences. As a result of her research and eloquent writings that captured public attention, the use of pesticides began to be controlled.

The Rachel Carson Refuge is a mix of forest and marshes, and home to more than 250 species of birds. Because marsh creeks weave in and out of the woodlands, visitors walk on boardwalks or hard-packed trails for most of the way. Deer, river otter, beaver, fox, coyote, moose, and harbor seals may be seen. The Refuge is home to several species of snakes (see sidebar, page 58), painted and spotted turtles, spring peepers, wood frogs, and salamanders. At several points, the trail leads into the open marsh, offering a breathtaking view of waving grasses, still waters, and egrets and herons stalking their food. There is a certain stillness about the Rachel Carson Refuge that casts a spell.

The Rachel Carson trail is fairly short, only about a mile, and easy going even for fairly young children. The trail is self-guided and brochures may be picked up at the Refuge office between 8:00 A.M. and 4:30 P.M., Monday through Friday, with limited hours on weekends and during summer. The trail itself is open daily from dawn to dusk. As with any of these trail walks, use of insect repellent is advised. Mosquitoes, black flies, and other biting flies (especially greenheads in the marsh areas) are common, and Lyme disease is present in Maine. The Refuge is accessible year-round, and offers excellent cross-country skiing come winter. For more information on the Refuge, call (207) 646-9226 or visit **http://rachel carson.fws.gov.**

If you would like to get closer to the water, then try your hand at fishing. Deep-sea fishing is available from Wells, but if you want to try something different, spend a few hours **surf casting** or **saltwater fly fishing.** The season runs from mid-May to mid-October and favorite spots include Wells, Drakes Island and Moody beaches, and the Wells breakwater. Fish for trophy-sized striped bass, bluefish, and sea-run brown trout. (One eight-year-old caught a 28-pound striped bass!) At the Wells Harbor town dock at high tide, families with children can easily catch harbor pollock, mackerel, small stripers, the occasional flounder, and small crabs. Other good fishing spots are any of the town jetties or one of the numerous bridges that cross the Ogunquit River. No fishing license is required in any of the tidewaters mentioned. Stop at the Wells Information Center on Route 1 for information on fishing gear rentals. The center is just past Bourne Avenue as you head north.

Wells Harbor can be accessed from either Mile Road or Drakes Island Road both off Route 1. (See earlier directions to Wells Beach and Drakes Island Beach. Remember, if you are visiting these locations after coming back from the Rachel Carson Refuge, the turns will now be on your left.) You can also take Harbor Road, which is on your right from Route 1 heading north, or on your left if you are heading south. To fish from the bridges spanning the Ogunquit River, head back south on Route 1 toward the Bourne Avenue turnoff. Just south of Bourne Avenue, Route 1 begins crossing the Ogunquit River. Several side roads may also provide fishing opportunities.

As noted earlier, the activities in Wells are not found in "loop" format, as most of them are right off Route 1. Our first journey up Route 1 took us to fishing spots, beaches, and reserves. We now repeat that journey north on Route 1, this time looking at other activities Wells has to offer.

One key characteristic of the Maine coast is its lighthouses and Wells is a good place to learn more about these historic landmarks. Your first stop should be the **Museum of Lighthouse History,** adjacent to the **Lighthouse Depot,** on Route 1. The Museum and Depot are on your left as you head north. You may have noticed them as you traveled up to the Laudholm Reserve. They can't be missed due to the large lighthouses on the front lawn! The museum contains rare artifacts of the U.S. Lighthouse Service and the U.S. Coast Guard, which was responsible for the upkeep, function, and staffing of many of the country's lighthouses. (Today, most of Maine's lighthouses are owned by the towns they are in, private individuals, or associations. The Coast Guard only maintains the lights and towers.) The museum is open year-round, free of charge. Call (207) 646-0245 for more information.

For a truly comprehensive look at lighthouse memorabilia, visit the **Lighthouse Depot.** This store claims to have the "world's largest" collection of lighthouse gift items. The Depot is a charter member of the American Lighthouse Foundation and works to promote the beauty and history of lighthouses. They have been featured in *Yankee Magazine,* national newspapers, and even on television spots. The store has thousands of lighthouse items for the serious collector or the visitor wanting a souvenir. Look for limited edition items, books, guides, videos, original art and handcrafts, posters, cards and prints, holiday ornaments, T-shirts and sweatshirts, and even home and garden furnishings.

Children will be fascinated by the Depot's highly detailed replicas of some of Maine's most famous lighthouses, which are built to scale and cover entire tables, and the 6-foot tall lawn lighthouses. (Be prepared for requests to bring one home!) The museum and the shop are good ways to learn a bit about Maine's lighthouses before visiting some real ones further up the road. The Depot is open year-round. Call (207) 646-0608.

Before leaving Wells, take a moment to step back in time at the **Wells Antique Auto Museum,** located on Route 1 on your right as you head north, just beyond the Mile Road turnoff. The Museum has more than eighty cars dating from 1900 to 1963, including New England's largest display of "Brass Era" vehicles. Look for a 1963 Studebaker Avanti, a 1949 Cadillac Fleetwood, and a 1907 Stanley Steamer. Children will enjoy the collection of antique nickelodeons, antique arcade games (yes, they played games back then!), toys, license plates, old-fashioned gas pumps, and more. Antique car rides are available, too, so take a day to "go motoring" the old-fashioned way. The Wells Auto Museum is open daily Memorial Day to Columbus Day. Call (207) 646-9064 for more information.

Two other historical stops give you an idea of the Wells of days past. On Route 1, just south of the Country Hill Motel, is the **Bridge of Flowers at Webhannet Falls Park.** The Bridge of Flowers is maintained by the Webhannet Garden Club and the Historical Society of Wells and Ogunquit to recognize the site where Edmund Littlefield, one of Wells' first settlers, established the first permanent sawmills on the banks of the Webhannet River in 1640 and 1641. The flowers are a mass of color and the falls are striking. The summer months provide the best garden viewing, although fall foliage adds a brilliant backdrop to the falls.

Schoolhouse Division No. 9 is located on Route 9, a bit off the regular route but worth a visit. The schoolhouse was built by the town between 1899 and 1901 on one-half acre of land at a cost of $848.72! The schoolhouse is a single classroom designed for one teacher to instruct 35 to 40 students from kindergarten through eighth grade. It is typical of how rural children of yesteryear were educated. These schools fulfilled an important mission, as they made sure even children in rural areas received an education. Because Maine has been such a rural state, schools often took in children from a broad area, sometimes even outside of town limits.

By 1953, all of the rural schools in Wells had closed, including Schoolhouse No. 9. Only a handful of one-room schools exist in the United States today, and a few are in Maine. Many of these early schoolhouses have disappeared, but the town of Wells voted to restore Schoolhouse No. 9 as part of its Bicentennial in 1976. The schoolhouse looks today much as it did a century ago. You will see students' desks, complete with inkwells and slate blackboards, a wood stove, the teacher's desk, a recitation bench, a dipper and pail for providing drinking water, and a "two-holer" toilet with no plumbing! Ask your children to think a moment about how their school compares with this one. Would they have liked this kind of school?

Schoolhouse Division No. 9 is open to the public on Thursdays from 1:30 P.M. to 4:00 P.M. in July and August. For more information, call the Wells Historical Society at (207) 646-4775. To reach the Schoolhouse, head north on Route 1 from Ogunquit; after you enter the town of Wells, turn left onto Routes 109 and 9—there is a set of lights at this junction. In a few miles, Route 9 splits off to the left. Continue on Route 9 (also called North Berwick Road) and the Schoolhouse is about five miles out.

The Kennebunks: Kennebunk and Kennebunkport

If you continue north on Route 1, then turn onto Route 9 on your right, you will pass the Rachel Carson Refuge and continue on into **Kennebunkport.** Kennebunkport is a working fishing port and also a charming village filled with quaint shops. The heart of Kennebunkport is picturesque **Dock Square,** which overlooks the Kennebunk River. The Square has been a thriving commercial center for more than two hundred years. In the 1700s and 1800s, Dock Square was stocked with wares for local shipbuilding and sea-going traders. Today, these historic buildings house gift shops, antique and art galleries, boutiques, and restaurants. Visitors enjoy not only shopping and dining, but also strolling the tree-lined streets and admiring the historic homes. If parents wish to browse the shops, youngsters also will find places to their liking. Kennebunkport has a number of neat toy shops, Christmas shops, ice cream parlors, and other kid-friendly stores.

This area has been featured in several books. Dock Square was cited in Booth Tarkington's 1930 story *Mirthful Haven*, which called Dock Square "Cargo Square," and historian/author Kenneth Roberts immortalized the region in his book *Arundel*.

Just across the river is the village of Kennebunk, whose waterfront section is called the **Lower Village.** The Lower Village and the Kennebunk beaches are touched upon here because of the proximity to Kennebunkport and easy access from Kennebunkport. There is more on the Village itself later in the chapter.

Kennebunk has a rich maritime heritage. In the days of sailing ships, the river banks teemed with shipbuilders. Four-riggers, schooners, and clipper ships were all built here, then launched into the river and off to sea. The harbor still bustles with activity today: recreational, commercial, and fishing boats all set sail here just as they did centuries ago. Take a stroll down to the marinas via a number of scenic walkways.

Like Kennebunkport, Kennebunk has a thriving dining and retail district, with shops and restaurants for every taste. While parents probably could shop for days in either community, children will be looking for something to do. One of the best stops for kids is the **Seashore Trolley Museum** on Log Cabin Road off Route 9. Turn onto North Street, on your left, after coming into Dock Square. You will cross the junction of several streets and North Street will become Log Cabin Road. Continue on Log Cabin Road; the museum is well marked. The museum has twenty-five trolleys and antique buses and offers a 3.5-mile ride through the woods and fields on a restored trolley. Visitors can see trolley restoration work underway, and shop in the museum store. The Seashore

Trolley Museum is open daily, rain or shine, late May through mid-October, and weekends only in early May and late October. Call (207) 967-2800, or visit www.trolleymuseum.org for more information. All aboard for a ride into the past!

On warm days, the ocean calls and it is never far away in the Kennebunks. The area abounds with **beaches.** For three of the most popular beaches, keep following Route 9 northeast, through Kennebunkport, and out past Cape Porpoise. Route 9 will become Mills Road at this point. Watch for Dyke Road or New Biddeford Road on your right. Either will lead you down to Goose Rocks Beach. **Goose Rocks Beach** is 3 miles long and very popular with those who like to walk for long stretches along the shore, and with younger children. It is a gentle swimming beach, and perfect for sand castles, picnics, tidepooling, and a nice lazy afternoon in the sun. The beach is wide, smooth, and sandy, and offers excellent views of Eastern Goose Rocks and Timber Island, just off the coast. A parking permit is required, which can be obtained at the Kennebunkport Police Station on Route 9, approximately 2 miles northeast of Dock Square, right by the school. There is a lifeguard at Goose Rocks Beach.

Arundel Beach or **Colony Beach**—so-called because it is near the Colony Hotel—is rockier. If you like to clamber about the rocks and tidepools hunting for marine life, or watch the surf kick up, Arundel Beach is an excellent choice. There is still a decent beach area for swimming, and no parking permit is required. From Route 9 in downtown Kennebunkport, turn right onto Ocean Avenue to access Colony Beach

Across the river from Colony Beach are **Kennebunk Beach, Middle Beach,** and **Gooch's Beach.** From Route 9 in the Lower Village of Kennebunk (before you cross the bridge to Kennebunkport), turn onto Beach Avenue on your right to reach them. All three are broad, sandy beaches with plenty of room for playing games, sunbathing, or just relaxing. There are lifeguards and public restrooms at both Gooch's Beach and Kennebunk Beach (which is also known as "Mother's Beach") from July through Labor Day.

Mother's Beach also has a playground, so if the kids tire of sun and surf, swings, slides, and other rides are right at hand. A sidewalk connects all three beaches, so it is easy to walk or jog from one to the other. A parking permit is required for any of these beaches and these can be obtained at either the Kennebunk Town Hall or Kennebunk Chamber of Commerce. The Kennebunk Town Hall is at 1 Summer Street, which is Route 35, the main road in Kennebunk. The Chamber of Commerce is on Western Avenue, which is Route 9, the road that brought you into Kennebunk and Kennebunkport.

The beaches are accessible year-round, but there are no services after Labor Day.

Most people associate beaches with the hot summer sun of afternoon, but a great time to explore is early morning or early evening, when the crowds have gone, and there is only the sea, the sounds of gulls, and the wide stretch of sand. The Kennebunks are unique in that they offer a number of **good beach walks.** The first one is the walk along Beach Avenue in Kennebunk, past Gooch's Beach and Mother's Beach, all the way to Lord's Point. It is a good stretch of the legs, but offers great views of shorefront homes and inns, as well as some spectacular ocean vistas.

In Kennebunkport, try the **Goose Rocks Beach shore walk.** It is a fine stretch of beach and particularly interesting to walk at low tide. Not only does this allow for great scavenging for shells, rocks, sea glass, and other "mysteries from the deep," it also allows you to see a barrier reef rock formation offshore known as "Goose Rocks." This phenomenon is so called because migrating geese are said to use this reef as a navigational point. (Follow the directions for Goose Rocks Beach to find the starting point of this walk.)

Also in Kennebunkport is the **Parson's Way** shore walk, which starts at Dock Square and leads down Ocean Avenue. This walk covers a bit of everything, from the stately Kennebunk River Green, to the town's historic homes and shops, to the busy marinas. As the ocean comes into view, Ocean Avenue becomes Parson's Way. You will notice the famous Colony Hotel on the left and Colony Beach on the right. During this first part of the walk, there are benches along the way so little legs can rest and everyone can enjoy the view. It is a great spot to enjoy the sunset.

Ocean Avenue now brings you to St. Ann's Church on your right, a spectacular stone church set right on the cliffs. The church and grounds are open to all, so take a moment to enjoy the view.

Just past St. Ann's Church, and almost in front of another landmark, Walker's Point, you'll see one of the area's great natural landmarks, **Spouting Rock.** On an incoming tide, and especially after a storm, the surf shoots up here in a great spout due to the unique rock formations. From Spouting Rock, look for **Blowing Cave,** down and to the right. The cave makes a roaring noise on an incoming tide or in times of high surf and also shoots up lots of spray.

After St. Ann's church and directly behind Spouting Rock is the famous estate now known worldwide as the "Summer White House." **Walker's Point** has been home to the Bush family for more than a century, and hence the summer vacation spot for two presidents, President George W. Bush (the forty-third president) and President George H. W. Bush (the forty-first president). It is not uncommon to see the Bush clan out fishing or boating, and President George Bush Sr. frequently comes to the Memorial Day ceremonies in Kennebunkport.

Younger children (under ten) will find the Parson's Way shore walk too long. The route is also very easy to drive, as you simply follow Ocean Avenue and Parson's Way as they weave along the shore. There are plenty of places to pull over and enjoy the view or get out to explore or stretch your legs.

The Parson's Way walk is also an excellent bike ride, but shore roads are not wide, so this is probably not a trek for younger children, but rather for twelve and up, with parental accompaniment. Whether walking or biking, you can either turn back after Walker's Point and retrace your route, or continue, looping up past Turbat's Creek, and returning to Dock Square through Wildes District Road and Maine Street.

After exploring the seashore, be sure to spend time visiting the village of **Kennebunk.** The town of Kennebunk is a true step back in time. You can reach Kennebunk by staying on Route 1 North from Wells and taking Route 35 on your right, or as Route 9 brings you into Kennebunkport, turn left onto Route 35. Adults will be especially taken by the town's beautiful tree-lined streets and amazing architecture. Homes, churches, and businesses in Colonial, Federal, Queen Anne, Greek Revival, and Italianate styles, dating from the mid-1700s to the 1800s line the streets. You will see the homes of the shipbuilders and sea captains who founded the town and the church where a bell cast by Paul Revere and Sons now hangs. Although younger children may be less interested in buildings, it is worth taking some time to let them discover this well-preserved slice of early America.

For a living history experience, visit the **Brick Store Museum** at 117 Main Street (Route 35) in Kennebunk. The Brick Store Museum encompasses four restored nineteenth-century buildings in the center of Kennebunk. Visitors journey from the time of the early settlers to the twenty-first century, thanks to changing exhibits, special programs, and workshops. The museum and its gift shop are open 10:00 A.M. to 4:30 P.M. Wednesday through Friday. For more information, call (207) 985-4802 or visit **www.brickstoremuseum.org**.

Young and old alike are intrigued by the **Wedding Cake House,** a stunning piece of architectural confection built around 1825. Located on Route 35, the Wedding Cake House was built by a sea captain as a substitute for a real wedding cake when he was called to sea. Since the house is privately owned, it generally is not open to the public, although sometimes appointments can be made for viewing the interior. In any case, quite a bit of the exterior and grounds are visible from the road and worth a look. Call (207) 967-0857 for more information. The Wedding Cake House is a few miles outside of downtown Kennebunk, on Summer Street (Route 35) as you head west toward Route 1. It is on the left-hand side, and cannot be missed, with its bright yellow coloring and elaborate trim. A sign labeled "The Wedding Cake House" is out front.

For an afternoon of arts, crafts, and special children's events, visit **River Tree Arts** on 35 Western Avenue in the waterfront section of Kennebunk known as Lower Village. Western Avenue is Route 9, the main road bringing you into Kennebunk's Lower Village and Kennebunkport. River Tree Arts is not far from the Brick Store Museum. For information on planned activities, visit **www .rivertreearts.org** or call (207) 967-9120. Something fun is happening at River Tree year-round.

Looking for outdoor activities? Kids will enjoy a wagon ride, horseback rides, and a chance to meet some friendly ponies at **Rockin' Horse Stables** on Arundel Road in Kennebunkport (Arundel Road is Route 9, the road you came into town on). For more information, call (207) 967-4288. Ever seen an alpaca up close? You can meet dozens of them at **Lightfoot Farms** at 29 Wakefield Road, off Route 99. Learn how wonderful yarn is made from their fleece, see the spinning mill, and visit the farm store. Call (207) 985-7629 or visit **www.lightfootfarms.com** for more information. To get there from Kennebunkport, follow signs for Route 1 to Kennebunk. Once in Kennebunk, take Route 1 south to the Dairy Queen, which will be on your right. From the Dairy Queen, follow signs for Route 99 West, Sanford. At the grassy triangle intersection, continue nine-tenths of a mile more on Route 99 West, then turn left onto Wakefield Road. Lightfoot Farms is on the right.

Do you know how toothpaste is made? Visit **Tom's of Maine** and watch them make toothpaste, lotion, soap, and other natural healthcare products. Tom's of Maine products are sold worldwide; the company specializes in wholesome products made with herbs and other plant products. Samples are available and you can make purchases at the store. Tom's of Maine is located in Lafayette Center on the Mousam River at the corner of Route 1 and Storer Street in Kennebunk. You will need to turn onto Storer Street to park. Call (207) 985-6331 or visit **www.toms-of-maine.com** for more information. (At this writing, Tom's of Maine manufacturing, and hence the tours, was planning to move to neighboring Sanford, Maine. The retail store, however, would remain in Kennebunk. If you wish to take a tour, definitely call first to verify the location.) The Tom's of Maine store and factory are both open year-round, although the factory is closed for all major holidays and weekends.

A great place to spend a morning or afternoon is the **Kennebunk Plains**. Follow Route 9 back west toward the junction of Route 1 and Route 9 in Wells. From there, go right, taking Route 1 North. Pick up Route 99 on your left from Route 1. The Kennebunk Plains are 1,100 acres of grasslands habitat protected by The Nature Conservancy. To see this kind of habitat in Maine is rare, as the state is largely heavily forested and hilly. This sprawling expanse is home to several rare and endangered species of wildlife and plants. The area is also known as the "blueberry plains," for the abundant blueberry bushes that bear fruit in July. Nothing beats the taste of a wild Maine blueberry.

The Plains are a favorite place for birdwatchers, as dozens of bird species are found here, including the endangered grasshopper sparrow. For a real treat, visit in August when the rare northern blazestar blooms, transforming the fields into a purple carpet. Ninety percent of the world's blazestar population is found here. Bring your camera!

The Plains are a wonderful place to hike, bike, explore, picnic, take pictures, and generally relax. The vistas are wide open, and roads lead you easily through the vast grasslands and scrub oak woods. There are ponds, abundant wildlife, and stunning wildflowers. Because this is a wild area, no restrooms or services are available. You may visit the Plains year-round, although access in winter would be difficult, as the roads are not plowed. Access is limited primarily to cross-country skiing.

If you want to rent a bike, visit the **Cape-Able Bike Shop,** at the corner of Log Cabin Road and Arundel Road (Route 9), about one-half mile from Dock Square in Kennebunkport. The shop offers a wide range of rentals, including mountain bikes, tandem bikes, bikes for kids, and Tag-Alongs. Among the makes available are Trek, Raleigh, Cannondale, and Santa Cruz. They can also service your bike if you have a problem. Call (207) 967-4382 for more information.

Both Kennebunks offer the full range of **deep-sea fishing cruises, recreational cruises,** and **whale-watch trips.** Half- or full-day options are available. Most cruises run Memorial Day to Labor Day. Some extend their season into the fall, but many base that decision on whether the fall is stormy and cold or sunny and pleasant. If you are visiting pre- or post-season, it is best to call first to see if the cruise you want is available.

For a couple of unique trips, check out the *Atlantic Explorer,* which offers two-hour trips departing from the Nonantum Resort on Ocean Avenue in Kennebunkport. The *Atlantic Explorer* sails past Walker's Point, Goat Island Light, and Cape Porpoise Harbor. Along the way, visitors not only will see seals and seabirds, but also will have an underwater view of life in the harbor and ocean thanks to an underwater video camera. It is a fascinating peek at the underside of Maine's coast. For more information, call (207) 967-4784 or visit **www.sceniccruise.com.**

The *Lady J* Sportfishing Charters provides a two-hour "discovery cruise" for kids. Families may fish for mackerel or help haul lobsters. Either way, the *Lady J* promises an educational, hands-on experience that kids will never forget. Call (207) 985-7304 for more information. The *Lady J* sails from the Arundel Wharf Restaurant off Ocean Avenue in Kennebunkport.

For the more adventurous family, **sea kayaking tours** are available through **Harbor Adventures** in Kennebunkport. All tours are led by a Registered Maine Guide, and instruction and equipment are provided. (Registered Maine Guides are men and women who have completed extensive study in nature craft and outdoor skills such as tracking, kayaking, canoeing, survival, and so forth. You have to be tested and licensed to be a Registered Maine Guide.) Paddle tours of various lengths are available. Call (207) 363-8466 for more information. In order to have a safe, satisfying paddle, Harbor Adventures will want to know the age and physical ability of the folks in your party. They will also ask about any previous kayaking or paddling experience. This will help them direct you to the tour that is right for you and your family. You will need to call Harbor Adventures in advance. Although they run trips out of the Kennebunks, their office is in York. They will direct you to a location after assessing your abilities and wishes.

Given the unpredictability of the Gulf of Maine, even harbor waters can be rough. Inexperienced paddlers may want to enjoy their first kayaking experience on one of the area's tidal creeks. Kayaking on a lake or stream is much different than kayaking in the ocean, where you are contending with currents, tides, eddies, and even whirlpools in some areas. Even those with some ocean background may be wise to take a refresher course or go with a guide until you become more familiar with the area. Sea kayaking is generally considered a sport for older children and adults.

If you do decide to kayak, you should bring sunscreen, a hat, sunglasses, and a jacket; wear water shoes or sneakers that can get wet; bring dry clothes in a waterproof bag, and drinking water. Depending on the length of the paddle, you may wish to bring food or snacks, also in a waterproof bag. If you bring cameras or binoculars, or any other equipment that you want kept dry and safe, pack it in something that is waterproof and floats. Many kayaks have safe storage compartments.

Visit the **Kennebunkport Marina** for canoe, kayak, skiff, and fishing rentals. The Kennebunkport Marina is at 67 Ocean Avenue, which is on your right as you head northeast, or call (207) 967-3411 for more information.

The kayaking and diving season for visitors is typically the summer months, when waters are calmer and warmer. Fall is a beautiful time to kayak, but seas can be rougher, so a trip on a stream or backwater may be safer and more pleasant. Again, discuss your ages, abilities, and experience with an experienced local guide from an outfit such as Harbor Adventures before venturing out. They can recommend a paddle destination that is safest for you, and provide a guide if need be.

If your family has experience **scuba diving,** then the Kennebunks are a great place to dive. Six shipwrecks lie between Mother's Beach, Kennebunk and Goat Island, and Cape Porpoise. One of the more shallow dives is off Mother's Beach, where the ribs of an old wooden vessel stick out of the sand. The maximum depth here is 20 feet.

Inside the mouth of Cape Porpoise lie two wrecks, the *Charles H. Trickey* and the *Mary E. Olys*. Both were blown onto the rocks off Goat Island Light during a raging winter storm back on January 1, 1920. The ships foundered within six hours of each other. The *Trickey* was carrying a load of boxboard out of Portland, Maine, to Lynn, Massachusetts, and the *Olys* was carrying granite from Stonington, Maine, to New York. The hulls were pounded to pieces and are a total loss. This is a very shallow dive just inside the mouth of the harbor; a boat is needed, though, to get to the site.

The other wrecks are in deeper water. For more information about the *Lively Lady, Schooner Empress* and *Wandby*, contact the local dive shop, **Divers Locker,** at (207) 985-3161. The Divers Locker is also a great place to get outfitted for diving if you do not have diving equipment with you, and to get any questions answered regarding diving requirements in Maine. They can assess the difficulty of visiting any of these wrecks. Any of these dives would primarily be for older children and teens with diving experience. Divers Locker is located at 460 Old North Berwick Road in Lyman. To get there, take Route 35 northwest, then bear left onto Walker Road, then turn left onto Old North Berwick Road.

Diving in this region is primarily a summertime activity. Experienced adult divers who are familiar with local waters may dive into the winter months, but fall and winter diving is definitely not an activity for children, novices, or those without some knowledge of the area. From October on, the waters of the Atlantic and its tributaries are extremely cold and seas often run high. Hypothermia and encounters with strong currents are very possible.

Before leaving the Kennebunks, be sure to visit **Cape Porpoise.** Cape Porpoise is technically part of Kennebunkport; it is the town's "other waterfront," the working waterfront where fishing, lobstering, and all the work of a traditional Maine seaport are still carried on. Cape Porpoise was discovered and named by Captain John Smith in the 1600s. Its good, sheltered harbor has long made it popular with fishermen and boat owners. Take a minute to enjoy this quiet harbor. Kids will be intrigued by the workings of the Cape—the boats arriving and departing, lobstermen and fishermen at work, gulls vying for a taste of the catch.

The Cape is home to some excellent seafood restaurants, a fish market, country grocery store, and shops and accommodations on a smaller scale.

To reach Cape Porpoise, continue northeast on Route 9 (the route that brought you into Kennebunkport from Route 1), and take Pier Road on your right. This brings you right down to the working harbor. If you wish to take the "scenic route" to Cape Porpoise, simply pick up Ocean Avenue on your right from Route 9 in downtown Kennebunkport. Ocean Avenue, as mentioned before, weaves along the coast. It eventually becomes Turbat's Creek Road, which leads you to Wildes District Road on your right. Wilde District Road brings you back up to Route 9. From Route 9, turn off onto Pier Road on the right.

While at the Cape, be sure to see **Goat Island Light.** Goat Island Light is best viewed from the Cape Porpoise Pier. Goat Island Light was first established in 1834 to guide mariners into the Cape Porpoise Harbor. In 1860, the stone tower and lightkeeper's house were rebuilt, and sometime between 1880 and 1890 the present 25-foot tower was constructed. Goat Island was the last Maine lighthouse to be automated. The last keeper was in 1990; the light is now automated and owned by the Kennebunk Conservation Trust. During President George Bush Sr.'s term, the lighthouse was called the "President's Light," as the Secret Service maintained an outpost there to guard the president.

If you visit the Kennebunks in August, make sure to catch the **Annual Teddy Bear Show and Sale,** which features hundreds of bears and collectors from all over the country. Call (207) 967-0857 for more information and this year's date. The Teddy Bear Show has typically been held at the Kennebunk High School, which is on Fletcher Street (Route 35). If you come into Kennebunk on Route 1 North, look for Route 35 west on your left; take 35 and head west. The school will be on your right, just before the tennis courts. If you journey to Kennebunk after visiting Kennebunkport, the directions are slightly different. From Route 9 in Kennebunkport, turn right onto Route 35 west and proceed as previously directed. Children of all ages (and plenty of adults) enjoy this "festival of the furry ones" in all their myriad sizes, shapes, colors, and expressions.

At Christmastime, come for **Kennebunkport's Christmas Prelude**, a ten-day holiday celebration, usually held the first two weeks in December. Santa arrives by lobster boat and the tree in Dock Square is decked with lobster buoys and other nautical items. There is a tree-lighting ceremony, caroling, parade, shopping specials, and refreshments. Call (207) 967-0857 or visit **www.christmasprelude .com** for more information and this year's date.

◢ More Lobster Lore

By the 1840s, lobstering had already begun to be a profitable business along the Maine coast. But, by the turn of the century, lobster was so plentiful that it began to be perceived as a poor man's food! It was often fed to prisoners, and some servants of summer folk rebelled at being served lobster so frequently and demanded other food. Today, all that has changed and nearly everyone views lobster as a special treat.

If you talk about lobsters, you need to know the language. Lobsters generally have a larger "crusher" claw and a smaller "cutter" claw. A "cull" is a lobster with only one claw. Sometimes lobsters lose their claws in fights or while escaping traps or predators.

A "short" is a lobster that is thrown back because it is too small to meet the legal limit, while "keepers" must meet the catch size limit. "Chick" lobsters weigh 1 to 1¼ pounds. Some folks think the smaller lobsters are sweeter, while others believe larger lobsters, say 2 pounds and up, are just as good. The best way to find out is to sample more than one size while you visit!

❧ Hunting for Shells

Most people think of Florida and southern beaches as prime shell-hunting territory, and these states do have a colorful abundance washed up on their shores. However, Maine beaches also offer good shell hunting, and this pastime is sure to intrigue all ages.

Maine shells don't typically come in the pinks and corals associated with tropical beaches. Maine mollusks, or shell-bearing animals, tend to live in homes that are white, gray, shades of brown, or bluish-purple. Following are some examples of shells you may find along the southern Maine coast. This is a very cursory overview, as Maine has an abundance of mollusk species and only the barest sampling is described here. For a complete guide, consult *Peterson's Guide to the Atlantic Seashore,* a wonderful "bible" for beach and tidepool exploration.

Razor clam. This clam has a white shell, up to 10 inches long, and narrow in width. It is shaped like an old-fashioned straight razor. Its shape, and the sharp edges of its shell, give the clam its name.

Soft-shelled clam. This clam has the classic large, saucer-shaped shell. It is white and about the size of an adult's palm. This is the clam Mainers choose for frying. It also is the clam that squirts at you from tidal flats. People collect this clam's shell to make wreaths (by hot-gluing the shells together, one layer overlapping the other) or to line cottage pathways. Children like the shell's broad, smooth surface for painting designs on, and sometimes turn the shells into the Asiatic saipan hats that they resemble.

Blue mussel. The small shells of this animal range from dark blue and white to blue and black, and even bluish-purple in color. They may be found singly, or as a cluster, and sometimes attached to seaweed. The inside of the shell is usually a lovely violet.

Horse mussel. Larger than the blue mussel, the outer coating of the horse mussel's shell tends to be more brownish-blue and flaky. The base of the shell is white tinged with mauve. The horse mussel is considered inedible.

Snails, periwinkles, dogwinkles, and whelks. There is an abundance of these mollusks in Maine, and a great variety within each species. These are all spiral-shelled animals. Their shells are typically shades of brown, brown and white, all white, or grayish-white—again, depending on the species. The snails and periwinkles tend to be less than an inch to 1 inch in size; the dog-winkles fall in the mid-range, while the whelks are the bigger animals, with their shells ranging from 1 to 7 inches in length.

Limpets. These little animals have the famous "eyeball" shells. Their small, round shells with scalloped edges are easily identified by the blue dot in a white circle—the "eyeball"—right in the center. The rest of the shell is usually brown and white.

Deep-sea scallop. Deep-sea scallops are not found in the intertidal zone, but pieces of their shells may be washed up by storms. The scallop is known by its classic fan-shaped shell, which is fairly flat and finely ridged. An intact shell can be up to 8 inches across, but finding a whole one is rare. The shells are usually an orange shade.

✒ *Maine Snakes*

Does Maine have any poisonous snakes? The verdict still seems to be out. Officially, Maine does not, but since some timber rattlers are found in New Hampshire, which borders Maine, it is not unlikely that a few reside in the Pine Tree State. Snakes, and other wildlife, seem to disregard official borders and chances are some have slithered over to the Maine side. However, it is safe to say that neither Maine (nor New Hampshire) have an abundant or widely dispersed population of timber rattlers, so the odds of encountering one are rare.

Maine is home to many species of snakes, among them the garter snake, milk adder, northern water snake, green snake, puff adder, rat snake, hognose snake, and others. Most of these are not typically aggressive. They usually prefer to be left alone, or make a quick exit. However, any wild animal can become aggressive if provoked or if it fears it is going to be harmed. Maine snakes do bite and the bite can be painful. The bite of any wild animal carries bacteria and would require a thorough cleaning and tetanus shot. If you see a snake, leave it alone. Do not try to pick it up, poke it with a stick, or otherwise disturb it. Let it lie. If one approaches you, move out of the way.

Snakes do a great deal of good, keeping rodent populations in check and playing a key role in the natural order of our ecosystems. For more information on snakes of Maine, contact the Maine Department of Inland

Fisheries and Wildlife at (207) 287-8000—they also offer a beautiful poster. A good guide for children is the Take-Along Guide, *Snakes, Salamanders and Lizards*. Although it is not a complete listing of all Maine snakes, it does feature a number of key species. It has colorful pictures and well-presented information. The facts about lizards and salamanders are also interesting. Note that not all the species listed are found in Maine, so be sure to read the habitat information carefully.

❧ *About Maine Guides*

Maine has a long history of outdoor guides. The state's heavily-forested interior and rugged coastline have encouraged outdoor pursuits such as fishing, hunting, canoeing, sea kayaking, and along with them, the need for expert guides. In Maine, a "guide" is anyone who accepts a fee for services in "accompanying or assisting anyone in the field, forest, waters or ice ... while hunting, fishing, trapping, boating, snowmobiling, or camping at a primitive camping area," according to the Maine Department of Inland Fisheries and Wildlife.

The first Maine Guide was licensed in 1897, and was a woman, "Fly Rod Crosby." That first year, seventeen hundred guides were licensed. At the time, guiding was primarily for hunters and fisherman. Big game hunting (bear and deer) was the mainstay of a guide's income, with fishing on inland lakes and streams a close second. Canoe trips were also starting to gain in popularity.

For many years, a Maine Guide was not required to pass any standardized test. Interested parties simply were reviewed by the local game warden and if they passed muster with him, they were considered fit to be a guide. (This was not as lax as it may seem, as most folks in rural communities knew each other, and most wardens had a pretty good idea of who was fit and who was not.)

As the number of guide applicants continued to grow, it became necessary to create a standardized test, and in 1975, the current system was launched. It requires a written and oral examination pertinent to the guide's stated area of expertise, such as sea kayaking, hunting, fishing, whitewater rafting, or recreation. (Certification is given only in these areas, and for whitewater rafting, the guides are registered for specific rivers.) The tests also require the guide to have expertise in navigation (map and compass on land), first aid, motor boat operation, survival skills, and rescue skills, among others. Most guides specialize in one area, but some have expertise in several areas and become certified as Master Guides.

There are currently four thousand Registered Maine Guides, and most are independent small businesses. They may work alone, or contract with sporting camps or other businesses. The Maine Professional Guides Association is comprised of Registered Maine Guides who are working to improve the criteria and ethics of the guiding industry. However, not all Registered Maine Guides are members of the Maine Professional Guides Association.

You may search for a Registered Maine Guide by town, company, or activities by visiting **www.maineguides.org**. Local town halls, sporting goods stores, sporting camps, and other outdoor venues often have this information as well.

Wells Highlights at a Glance

- Wells beaches
- Wells Reserve at Laudholm Farm: (207) 646-1555
- Rachel Carson National Wildlife Refuge: (207) 646-9226
- Surf casting and fly fishing
- Museum of Lighthouse History: (207) 646-0245
- Lighthouse Depot: (207) 646-0608
- Wells Antique Auto Museum: (207) 646-9064
- Bridge of Flowers at Webhannet Falls: (207) 646-4775
- Schoolhouse Division No. 9 (Wells Historical Society): (207) 646-4775
- Wells Chamber of Commerce: (207) 646-2451

Kennebunk and Kennebunkport Highlights at a Glance

- Dock Square
- Lower Village
- Seashore Trolley Museum: (207) 967-2800
- Goose Rocks Beach
- Colony or Arundel Beach
- Kennebunk or Mother's Beach
- Middle Beach
- Goose Rocks shore walk
- Parson's Way shore walk
- Spouting Rock
- Blowing Cave
- Walker's Point (Summer White House)
- Brick Store Museum: (207) 985-4802
- Wedding Cake House: (207) 967-0857
- River Tree Arts: (207) 967-9120
- Rockin' Horse Stables: (207) 967-4288
- Lightfoot Farms: (207) 985-7629
- Tom's of Maine: (207) 985-6331
- Kennebunk Plains
- Cape-Able Bike Shop: (207) 967-4382
- *Atlantic Explorer:* (207) 967-4784
- *Lady J* Sportfishing Charters: (207) 985-7304
- Harbor Adventures: (207) 363-8466
- Kennebunkport Marina: (207) 967-3411
- Divers Locker (for shipwreck information): (207) 985-3161
- Cape Porpoise
- Goat Island Light
- Annual Teddy Bear Show: (207) 967-0857
- Christmas Prelude: (207) 967-0857
- Kennebunk and Kennebunkport Chamber: (207) 967-0857

For an attraction-filled visit, this is the area: Funtown/Splashtown, Palace Playland, Aquaboggan Water Park, Pirates Cove Adventure Golf—they are all here. But attractions are not all the area has to offer. Area parks offer hundreds of acres of nature trails, many near the shore. Paddle a canoe through Scarborough Marsh. Go picnicking or hiking. Race a go-cart. Swim and play on Old Orchard's famous seven-mile beach, and come evening, stroll the famous pier.

Biddeford and Saco

Route 1 North from Kennebunk leads you through the small cities of **Biddeford** and **Saco.** The two communities are twin cities, similar in character and history, and separated only by the Saco River. Because of their close proximity and shared qualities, the area is frequently referred to as "Biddeford/Saco."

The Biddeford/Saco area is one of the quieter parts of the Maine coast. Both are former mill towns, as evidenced by the many large, red brick buildings lining their streets. Most of the mills were cotton mills, but there were also nail factories, iron foundries, machine shops, and cigar factories. The cities had 10 miles of riverfront, 10 miles of oceanfront, and good harbors, making them ideal for industry. They also shared the dramatic falls of the Saco River, which were harnessed by massive cotton mills in the 1800s. Given their location and the commitment of a hard-working population, the cities of Biddeford and Saco were manufacturing leaders during the industrial age.

This industry strongly influenced the cities' culture. The mills employed thousands of immigrant workers, largely from Europe and Quebec. Even today, there is a strong French-Canadian influ-

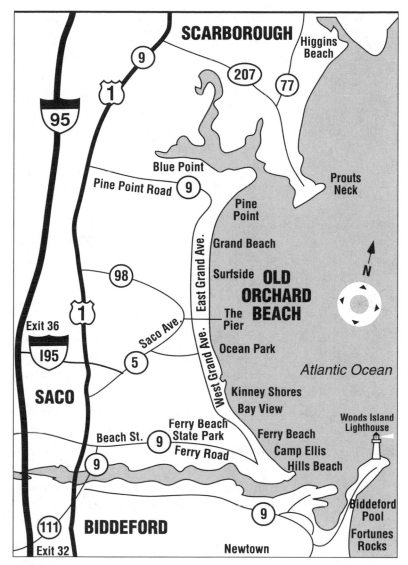

Biddeford, Saco, Old Orchard Beach, and Scarborough
Wild beaches, famous beaches, rocky shores, lighthouses, nature preserves, plus one of
Maine's most beloved amusement parks at Old Orchard Beach—they're all found in this
section of southern Maine. *Map by Denise Brown of Ad-Cetera Graphics.*

ence. The mills survived the Civil War, the Panic of 1873, and the Crash of 1929, and prospered into the mid–twentieth century. They became famous for their sheets and pillowcases, blankets, towels, and accessories. Eventually, the cotton mills began to die out as more products were produced overseas and synthetics came into vogue. Today, the industry of Biddeford and Saco is more diverse. Textile manufacturing still takes place (the area is home to the famed West Point Pepperell, now known as West Point Stevens, Inc.), but products such as plastics, electronics, metals, and composite materials are also being made. Tourism is gradually playing a bigger role, and Biddeford is now home to a state-of-the-art marine research facility.

Part of the draw for tourists is the area's **beaches.** Although these beaches are less well-known than some others on the southern coast, Biddeford and Saco actually have some of the finest beaches in Maine. All of the beaches are accessible year-round, but with no services before Memorial Day or after Labor Day. From Route 1 North in Biddeford, pick up Route 111 East on your right, then turn onto Routes 9 and 208, also on your right; these routes lead to the beaches. As you head south along Route 208, look for **Beach Avenue** and **Hills Beach** on your left. Hills Beach is a small (530-yards), sandy beach with limited parking, and no facilities. Parking is by permit, which can be obtained at the city clerk's office at city hall at 205 Main Street (Route 9). At this writing, the hours for the city clerk's office were Mondays 8:00 A.M. to 5:00 P.M., Tuesdays 8:00 A.M. to 7:00 P.M., and Wednesdays through Fridays 8:00 A.M. to 5:00 P.M. Call (207) 284-9307 for more information. As you continue south on Routes 208 and 9, you will next come to Biddeford Pool on your left. Route 208 leads you right down to the lovely 2-mile stretch of beach at the sheltered cove known as **Biddeford Pool.** There are lifeguards and bathhouses at Biddeford Pool but no other services, and a parking permit is required. Biddeford Pool is a community with two faces. It is known for its marshes (great birdwatching), lupines (a tall, bluish-purple wildflower blooming in June), and stately, elegant homes. Yet it is a true working harbor, with weathered fishermen's homes lining the shore and boats bobbing at anchor.

Take Route 208 North back to Route 9 and go left, heading southwest on Route 9. This brings you to **Fortune's Rocks Beach** on your left. This beach is a good sandy expanse that has lifeguards and facilities, and also requires a parking permit, again obtainable at the city clerk's office.

The final beach in the area is not part of the Route 208 loop, yet it is easily accessible. **Rotary Park Beach** is on Main Street in Biddeford. If you are just entering Biddeford on Route 1 North, turn left onto Main Street; Rotary Park Beach will be on your right. If you are coming up from the Biddeford Pool area, then head northeast on Route 208 to Route 9. At the junction of Route 111, turn right onto Route 9 North, then left onto Main Street. You will come to Rotary Park Beach on your right.

Rotary Park Beach on the lower Saco River offers a slightly different experience, as it is tidal river and not the ocean. There is a nice, sandy beach, lifeguards, and free parking. The park spans 83 acres and includes ball fields, a boat launch, a playground, and picnic and barbecue facilities.

In Saco, the choices are equally varied. After Route 208 loops back to Route 9, continue following Route 9 northeast and you will cross the Saco River. Continue east on Route 9, toward the coast, to reach the Saco area beaches and parks. The first beach you will come to is **Camp Ellis,** which is right on Route 9 and has a 2,000-foot sandy beach. There is one good-sized public parking lot with no fee; other parking in the area does have a fee. There are no restrooms or other facilities. For food, most locals visit two popular and long-established restaurants—**Huots** and **Wormwoods,** which are both right near the beach. The food is casual, good, and available for takeout. Portions of Camp Ellis have been the scene of some spectacular surf during and after storms. The eroding effect of this surf has been featured on the Weather Channel's "Storm Stories" program.

As you head northeast on Route 9, watch for **Bay View Beach** and **Kinney Shores.** These are small, sandy beaches that are perfect for families. Both Bay View Beach and Kinney Shores have lifeguards and free parking. (Remember, lifeguards and facilities are seasonal; after Labor Day, there is no guarantee that either will be present. If there are a few warm weekends in early September, lifeguards may be on duty, but that is not usually the case.) The beaches are accessible for walking and exploring year-round. All of these beaches generally offer gentle surf and are fine for younger swimmers.

For something special, visit **Ferry Beach State Park,** a sheltered, sandy beach with natural sand dunes. (This is a different location from Ferry Beach in Scarborough, described later in this chapter.) Ferry Beach State Park covers 117 acres and offers nature trails, restrooms, and picnic areas. The nature trails are easy walking and a summer stroll takes you through lush forests, passed ponds filled with water lilies, and through areas lined with sweet-smelling bayberry bushes. The swimming beach is located across the road, but a walking tunnel leads you safely across. If you wish to go swimming with little ones, make a bathroom trip before you

Water lily pond at Ferry Beach State Park.

head to the beach, as all facilities are on the non-beach side of the road. This beach also offers gentle surf perfect for younger swimmers.

Parking is plentiful but there is a fee to use the state park. Ferry Beach State Park is on Bay View Road, which will be on your left as you head north on Route 9. The signage for the park is easily visible. Ferry Beach State Park's regular season is Memorial Day to Labor Day, but it may be open with services some weekends up through foliage season (mid- to late October.). The park is accessible year-round for hiking and cross-country skiing, although there will be no services and parking may be outside the gate.

Although Biddeford and Saco are small cities, some outstanding nature preserves are located within their boundaries. In Saco, consider visiting the **Saco Heath,** which encompasses 800 acres of nature trails. The property is managed by The Nature Conservancy. The Heath features a wealth of unique plant life, and because the area is quite wild, is home to abundant wildlife. Tracks of deer, raccoon, and even black bear may be seen. The Saco Heath is hard to find, and your best bet is to obtain directions locally—ask for Heath Road or Route 112.

Older children may appreciate the Heath's wildness, but younger children will find it overwhelming. Trails are easy to walk but lengthy. It would be a good mountain biking area (mountain biking is permitted, but please stay on the trails). There are no facilities of any kind, and no trail guides, but the area is abutted by other residences. Bug spray is a must. There are no official season dates for the Heath, although winter access could be tricky in terms of parking availability.

In Biddeford, visit **East Point Sanctuary** in Biddeford Pool on Route 208. From Route 9, pick up Route 208 East and follow this down to the Pool, which is a large, rockbound cove. The East Point Sanctuary is managed by the Maine Audubon Society, and covers 30 acres. This is a spectacular preserve, but again hard to spot. As you drive down to where Route 208 seems to dead-end, look sharp for the Audubon sign on your left. You may notice cars pulled over to the side of the road while the occupants either watch the surf or

An ocean view at East Point Sanctuary at Biddeford Pool.

visit the preserve. The entrance to the Sanctuary is a dark, green tunnel of vegetation, but it then opens up to an easy, open trail.

Once in the preserve, you will enjoy breathtaking ocean vistas of a wide expanse of sea, surf on the rocks, boats, and even Wood Island Light. There are wild roses and other abundant plant life, and a good amount of wildlife, especially birds. This is a good, easy walk for all but the youngest children. You can also tidepool, although little ones might need help getting down to the pools. You can walk the entire loop, or double back if that proves too long. At some points, as you head away from the shore, the trail becomes thick with vegetation on either side. Walking is still easy, but take care not to brush up against the poison ivy that is present in places. The Sanctuary is open year-round and is free of charge. There are no facilities.

For a touch of the Wild West, visit **Brush Brook Stables** at 463 West Street in Biddeford. Go right off Route 1 at the five corners intersection and you are on West Street. This intersection is in the center of town and unmistakable. Brush Brook Stables is home of the Ever After Mustang Rescue Training and Education Center. The Center takes in mustangs that need gentling and training. Although mustangs come from the West, many have found their way east through a succession of owners or auctions. Many of the horses have never been socialized or put under saddle. Because of this, they have a hard time finding good homes. At Brush Brook, they receive the training and gentling they need, and when ready, are placed in the homes they deserve. You can meet these mustangs and see the training process at the stables. The stables also offer trail rides and riding lessons. Call (207) 284-7721 or visit **www .mustangrescue.org**, for more information, and to see a profile of some of their horses.

Biddeford is also the site of one of Maine's more storied lighthouses, **Wood Island Light,** at the mouth of the Saco River. The 42-foot light tower marks the entrance to the harbor. The light was authorized by Thomas Jefferson and built in 1808; it was the thirteenth lighthouse to be built in the United States. The Friends of Wood Island Lighthouse have protected the light and begun its restoration. The lighthouse has a storied past. In its two hundred years, it has seen murder, suicide, explosions, military target practice, heroics, humor, and shipwrecks. A colorful cast of characters have touched the island, including rumored ghosts!

One ghost is believed to be that of a young man from the 1800s who killed himself on the island after accidentally shooting a lobsterman/deputy sheriff who also lived there. The young man had been drinking and pulled a gun on the sheriff. When the sheriff tried to disarm him, the gun went off and the sheriff was killed. When the young man sobered up and realized what had happened, he turned the rifle on himself. Since then, keepers and visitors to the lighthouse have sensed a presence and seen a ghostly figure. The ghost seems friendly, and most of his actions are more mischievous than mean—he opens and shuts supposedly locked doors, raises window shades, and makes sudden banging noises. Former keepers learned to accept him as one of the crew but never quite got used to seeing a locked door unlatch and open by itself.

One of the lighthouse's more beloved residents was Sailor, a collie/sheepdog mix, the pet of lighthouse keeper Thomas Henry Orcutt. Sailor would ring a salute on the fog bell to any craft who sounded their ship's whistle or bell as they passed the island. Sailor would grab the cord attached to the fog bell in his strong teeth and give a good hard pull. For years, fishermen and others looked forward to Sailor's greeting.

Wood Island Light is easily seen and photographed from the Biddeford Pool area (see previous directions), or from the Saco River (Hills Beach area, for example). For more information on the lighthouse and its stories, visit **www.woodislandlighthouse.org**.

One cannot visit this area without spending some time on the great **Saco River.** The Saco River is one of the most canoed and kayaked rivers in Maine. Stretching 121 miles from the mountains of New Hampshire to the ocean of Maine, the Saco offers spectacular views throughout its length, 10 miles of which run through Saco and Biddeford. However, paddlers need to be well-acquainted with the river's changing mood. In the lower stretches, the river can be a nice, placid paddle, but in its upper reaches, it has a strong current and whitewater runs. These whitewater segments are an exciting challenge for the experienced paddler, but not recommended for the inexperienced or those with children. Every year, lives are lost on the Saco by paddlers who get more river than they bargained for.

If you are looking for a safe section on which to enjoy some nice canoeing, book a **guided tour.** Many of the tours start farther north. Two good tours to look into are **Maine's River Run Canoe** tours and rental, or **Saco River Canoe and Kayak.** River Run is out of Brownfield, Maine, and Saco River Canoe and Kayak is out of Fryeburg; both are about an hour inland from the Saco/Biddeford area. You will find an enjoyable day of picnicking, swimming, and fishing with either tour. (You will need to bring your own rod and bait to fish.) Half- and full-day paddles are available. For River Run, call (207) 452-2500 or visit **www.riverruncanoe.com** for more information. For Saco River Canoe and Kayak, call (207) 935-2369 or visit **www.sacorivercanoe.com**. To reach either of these tours, take Exit 48 from Interstate 95 North, and follow Route 25 west to Route 113 West. Both are on Route 113.

For outdoor entertainment of a different kind, take in Saco's **Aquaboggan Water Park** and **Funtown/Splashtown USA**. Both are located right on Route 1 as you head north, and both attract healthy crowds during the summer. The best times to catch all the rides without lines are early in the day or early evening. **Funtown** has rides to please both older and younger children. Little ones will want to ride the merry-go-round, kiddie cars, kiddie canoes, boats, train, and a host of other gentler rides. There are also adult bumper boats and kiddie bumper boats. Everyone will enjoy the antique car rides and miniature golf. Older children will be clamoring to go on the roller coasters (yes, they have *two* coasters, including Maine's only wooden roller coaster!), trapeze ride, bumper cars, and several of their newer attractions—the Dragon's Descent and Thunder Falls Log Flume ride. Dragon's Descent takes riders up 200 feet in the air then drops them in a rapid free fall. You can find the location of Dragons Descent by the screams! The Thunder Falls Log Flume ride is essentially a roller coaster in water; it is New England's longest and tallest flume ride. Visitors ride in a simulated log down a river, then climb a large slide, swooshing down the other side. Be prepared to get wet!

Splashtown, the water park segment of Funtown, offers wading pools, wave pools, various water slides, and the signature ride, Pirate's Paradise, which is a series of water slides leading you to a platform where a giant bucket shaped like a pirate's head is continuously filled with water and dumped on the riders. This is one sure way to cool off!

There are restrooms and refreshment stands at both venues. You may buy tickets to only Funtown, only Splashtown, or a combination ticket to both. Many options are available. Funtown/Splashtown offers a number of discount days through the summer, many of them tied to offers at Hannaford Supermarkets and through Hershey products. Grab a brochure at the Saco Chamber of Commerce for full details; call (207) 284-5139 or visit **www.funtownsplashtown usa.com** for this summer's specials. The brochure is worth getting, as it typically includes a number of coupons good at the park and at area restaurants. Offers may be for discounts on pizza, burgers, candy bars, and other good deals for families. Both venues have a number of requirements regarding height of riders for certain rides, children being accompanied by an adult, and so on. Call or visit the web site for complete details.

Funtown begins its season with weekend openings in mid-May. It opens daily for the regular season in June, and remains open through July and August. There are also evening hours, but these vary by month and day of week, so visit the web site or call first. Funtown reverts to weekends-only through mid-September.

Splashtown starts its season in June, and follows the Funtown season, although evening hours usually end at 6:00 P.M. All hours are weather permitting. If it is a cool day, showery, or with thunderstorms forecast, you might want to call first.

On the whole, both parks are clean and well-cared for. They are large enough to cater to diverse interests and ages, yet small enough so visitors don't feel overwhelmed.

The **Aquaboggan Water Park,** also on Route 1, is another popular summer spot. Here, too, there are rides for all ages. The park has a wave pool, water slides of varying speed, and a toddler splash area. There is also miniature golf and mini-car racing. Aquaboggan is open mid-June to Labor Day. Call (207) 282-3112 for more information.

Funtown/Splashtown and the Aquaboggan Water Park are easily visible and well marked as you head north on Route 1.

Don't be surprised if you hear French spoken in Saco and Biddeford, or see Canadian flags flying. There is a strong French-Canadian influence here and folks are proud of their heritage. This pride is evident in full force in June when Biddeford hosts the **La Kermesse Franco-Americaine Festival,** the largest Franco-American festival in New England. The four-day festival typically starts on a Thursday with a block party and fireworks. Friday features a parade, and the weekend is filled with a carnival, musical entertainment, field events, and plenty of food and children's activities. For this year's date and more information, call (207) 282-2894.

Old Orchard Beach

Route 1 continues to be your passport to more fabulous beaches. From Route 1, take Route 5 East to **Old Orchard Beach.** No place in Maine compares with Old Orchard Beach for length and breadth of beaches. Seven miles of wide, glistening sands spread along this town's coastline. Old Orchard Beach is a mecca for beach-loving families from all over. It perfectly captures the traditional New England beach experience: children splash in the waves or race along the shore; the smells of fried dough and popcorn mingle with the salt air; couples stroll along the famous pier, occasionally stopping at its shops and eateries. In the distance, the Ferris wheel and other rides beckon. Come nightfall, Old Orchard Beach sparkles as its amusement park comes to life and fireworks splash the sky with color.

Old Orchard Beach was settled back in 1653. In its early years, the community took its name from the "old" apple orchard that stood on high land above the beach and served as a landmark to sailors. In 1837, an Old Orchard resident, E. C. Staples, was coaxed into taking summer boarders at his farm for $1.50 a week. Staples became convinced of Old Orchard's potential as a summer resort and built the first Old Orchard boarding house near the top of today's Old Orchard Street. The historic building is now the Old Orchard Inn.

Staples was right in his prediction, and in 1842, the first real wave of tourists arrived thanks to the new steam railroad running from Boston to Portland, with a station just 2 miles from town. The first restaurant to sell seafood treats and "shore dinners" (that popular Maine staple of lobster, steamers, corn, cole slaw, rolls, and blueberry pie) opened in 1851. During the Civil War, the area grew and grew, adding streets, stores, homes, stables, and hotels. By 1873, the Boston & Maine Railroad passed right through Old Orchard Beach and its place as a summertime destination was assured. (Rail service ended for a time, ceasing in 1923. Today the trains run once more, having resumed in 2001, and the new Boston & Maine train, the Downeaster, once again stops at the same location, the railroad depot having become the town's Chamber of Commerce.)

Over the years, Old Orchard has been the scene of many exciting events. In 1902, the first amusement center opened, complete with roller skating, merry-go-round, rides, games, and refreshments. In 1907, much of the waterfront burned but was quickly rebuilt, this time with a large standpipe to assure adequate water. In 1910, an international auto race was held on the wide sands, with Dave Lewis winning the 100-mile race. Auto races had been occurring at Old Orchard Beach since at least 1903, but by 1906, the area was attracting nationally ranked drivers. Many of the races were sprints, averaging about one mile in length, but longer distances were also contested, as noted earlier. All races started and ended at the pier. Grandstands were erected along the beach and the crowd roared as the cars raced down and back (sometimes several times, depending on the length of the race) along the sands. For a time, Old Orchard Beach was acclaimed as one of the finest and most competitive auto racing surfaces in the world, and as many as fifty thousand people packed the stands for big-name events. Auto racing began to wane by 1913 or so, as man-made tracks, where racing conditions could be more easily managed, came into vogue.

Adventurer seekers took to the skies as well as the sands at Old Orchard Beach. Sparked by Lindbergh's daring flight, many would-be transatlantic flights took advantage of Old Orchard's broad, packed sand to attempt their own crossings. Throughout the 1920s and '30s, the 2.5-mile strip of beach north of the pier became the departure point for a series of daring flying efforts. Old Orchard Beach was deemed perfect for these attempts because of the length of its "runway" and the geographic proximity of southern Maine to Europe. For a transatlantic flight or longer, planes were burdened with hundreds of extra gallons of gas. This extra payload meant they needed much longer runways in order to build up speed for take-off. A typical runway of the day was only about 3,000 to 4,000 feet long—not enough for a fuel-heavy plane. A long ribbon of beach fit the bill perfectly. Old Orchard Beach was also perfectly located. At the time, it was the most northeasterly airstrip in the United States, making it 100 miles closer to Europe than airfields in southern New England or New York.

Most of these attempts were not successful, but many were spectacular in the trying. The plane "Old Glory" nearly clipped the pier as it failed to build altitude fast enough; the craft later crashed off Newfoundland. Wealthy New York businesswoman Frances Wilson Grayson sought to become the first woman to cross the Atlantic. She took off in the ill-fated "Dawn," only to crash off Stratton Island, 3 miles from the beach, due to an overloaded plane. Shaken but unfazed, she tried again a few weeks later but had to put down in Nova Scotia due to mechanical trouble. In December, she and her co-pilot made one more attempt, this time taking off from New York, but the "Dawn" went down for good off Cape Cod. No trace of the plane or its pilots was ever found.

In August 1931, the famed barnstormers Wiley Post and Harold Gatty landed at Old Orchard Beach in their single-engine plane "Winnie Mae." They had just flown around the world in eight days. Two years later, Post would achieve another milestone when he circumnavigated the globe by himself.

An excellent book on Old Orchard's colorful history is *The Great Steel Pier* by Peter Dow Bachelder. It is available at most southern Maine bookstores and sold abundantly at Old Orchard Beach.

Today, **Old Orchard Beach** is packed full of family activities. The beaches alone lend themselves to picnics, kite flying, games, swimming, body surfing, building sand castles, and relaxing. Surf is low, so this is a great swimming beach for kids. The beach community makes sure that everything is family friendly. If you are hungry, lots of different food is available just steps from the beach— pizza, French fries, hot dogs, cheeseburgers, cotton candy, ice cream, soda—all the summertime favorites are here. If you want something more substantial, there are a range of family-style restaurants around the town.

Old Orchard's Pier is the center of things—visually, historically, and as an activity base. This 500-foot pier extends well out into the ocean and features shops, food stands, games of skill, and nightlife. The first pier was built in 1898. It was made of steel and measured 1,770 feet long and stood 20 feet above the tides. Unfortunately, it was damaged in November of that same year by a storm. In March of 1909, another great storm destroyed "White City" at the end of the pier and reduced the pier's length to 700 feet. During the 1920s and 1930s, all the "Big Bands" played the Pier Casino and thousands danced over the waves under the revolving crystal ball. Guy Lombardo, Rudy Valle, Duke Ellington, and many others from that era's famous dance bands came to the glistening sands and glittering nightlife of Old Orchard Beach. In 1978, one of the state's biggest blizzards nearly demolished the pier as record waves crashed over it. A new pier was immediately planned and soon constructed. The present pier was built in 1980 and so far, has withstood storm and tide.

Right on the beach is **Palace Playland,** Old Orchard's premier amusement park. Palace Playland has a giant arcade, beautiful carousel, Ferris wheel, roller coasters, Kiddieland, and much more. Test your skill at one of two hundred electronic games or feel the force of 70,000 gallons of water propelling you on a wild ride down the Log Flume, one of the most thrilling rides in the region. Enjoy a breathtaking view of the ocean and beach from the top of the 75-foot Gondola Sunwheel, the tallest Ferris wheel in New England. This ride is a great experience, day or night. The old-fashioned carousel has a unique collection of horses and other animals to ride and is one of the great traditions of this beachfront park. Hop aboard! It is fun for all ages.

Older children will clamor to experience the Power Surge, which lifts you more than 50 feet in the air, then turns you 360 degrees. Need more thrills? Try the five-story drops and turns of the Galaxi roller coaster, or the accelerated corners and spiral turns of the Orient Express, or maybe a fiendishly fast ride on the Tornado. Younger children will enjoy Kiddieland with its swirling teacups, splashing whale, mini motorcycle, and convoy truck rides. The whole family will enjoy the fireworks show, held every Thursday night at dusk. Palace Playland also offers a midway, gift shops, and refreshments. Admission is free. A variety of ride packages are offered, or you may purchase individual tickets. Palace Playland is open seven days a week from Memorial Day through Labor Day, with evening hours. For complete dates, times and ticket information, visit **www.palace playland.com**, or call (207) 934-2001.

Another great outdoor playground is the **Pirates Cove Adventure Golf,** located at 70 First Street in the heart of the beach district. From Route 5 East, turn right onto Orchard Street, then right again onto First Street. First Street runs parallel to West and East Grand Avenue (Route 9), which follows the beach. Pirates Cove is an outstanding miniature golf course, with thirty-six championship holes. Golfers play through shipwrecks, water falls, caves filled with treasure, and other themes from pirate lore. Pirates Cove is typically open from Memorial Day through Labor Day, but may be open weekends in May and early fall. For more information, call (207) 934-5086.

On Monday and Tuesday nights during the summer season, stop by the **Old Orchard Beach town square,** by the pier, for a **free concert.** Concerts start at 7:00 P.M. For a summer schedule, contact the Old Orchard Beach Chamber of Commerce at (207) 934-2500. Events are happening all summer long at the Beach, and even into the fall and winter. Check out the **Annual Car Show** in September, with numerous types of cars, parades, entertainment, and an evening party. It is great family fun. At **Christmastime,** there is the tree-lighting, with hayrides, entertainment, hot chocolate, food, a holiday bazaar, and Santa and Mrs. Claus arriving by fire engine. Before visiting, check out the Chamber's web site at **www .oldorchardbeachmaine.com** to see what is planned this season.

Old Orchard does have a quieter side, and it is found in the sister communities of **Pine Point** and **Ocean Park.** A mile south of the Pier is **Ocean Park,** a classic seaside resort community. Simply follow Route 9, also called West Grand Avenue, east from Old Orchard to reach Ocean Park. Ocean Park is the place to go for tennis and shuffleboard courts, concerts, a classic ice cream soda, or a walk along lovely nature trails. For that ice cream soda, stop in at the soda fountain in the center of town at Temple Park, which still serves the same sweet, homemade ice cream that it did a century ago. All of Ocean Park is a State of Maine Game Preserve with several walking trails through massive pine groves. Many of the Ocean Park activities (such as shuffleboard, concerts, and tennis) are geared for the summer season, but the walking trails are enjoyable year-round.

Three miles north of the pier, and also on Route 9, is **Pine Point,** another quiet vacation community. Pine Point sits at the mouth of the Scarborough River, just a few miles from the Scarborough Marsh Nature Preserve (see page 79). The town is home to gift shops, restaurants, and lobster pounds. There is a quiet beach, but it is largely private.

While in Old Orchard, you may notice that signage, menus, and other items are bilingual, and you may hear a touch of Français in the air. Old Orchard is a very popular spot with French-Canadian tourists who come down from Montreal and Quebec City. This beach resort has been a summer destination for them since the 1850s, when the Grand Trunk Railroad opened, connecting Montreal to Old Orchard, and allowing visitors from the north to flock to this wide, sandy beach.

Scarborough

Continue east on Route 9 (also called East Grand Avenue in Old Orchard Beach) to the town of **Scarborough.** Scarborough offers great diversity when it comes to things to do. Want to see a life-size chocolate moose? This is the place. How about a swim at any one of four beaches? Scarborough has them. Does canoeing through a wild marsh sound like a good afternoon adventure? Or, maybe you would like to hear the roar of the racetrack—from horses to stock cars and go-carts, Scarborough has them.

Most Maine visitors want to head for the water, and Scarborough has plenty to offer. Routes 9 and 207 will lead you to most of the beaches, marshes, and nature preserves.

As you journey east on Route 9, watch for Ross Road on your left. It is worth taking this slight detour to see an **Elk Farm.** The privately owned farm is just a few miles down the road. Elk meat is very popular and is being featured more and more frequently in restaurants and specialty markets. Most elk meat is imported from out west, but elk and buffalo farms are starting to appear in the East. This farm is generally not open to the public, but it is worth stopping to take a look at the animals and take a few pictures.

After viewing the elk, take Ross Road back to Route 9 and again head northeast. Up first is the **Scarborough River Wildlife Preserve and Bird Sanctuary,** which is managed by the Maine Audubon Society and covers 56 acres. The Sanctuary is on Route 9, also called Pine Point Road, about 2 miles before you reach Route 1. The Sanctuary has 1.5 miles of trails, and is perfect for hiking or cross-country skiing come winter. The Preserve is accessible year-round. Call (207) 883-8427 for more information.

Next stop is the **Scarborough Marsh Nature Center,** which is well marked and on your right as you continue northeast on Route 9. Scarborough Marsh is an Audubon Preserve, and at 3,100 acres, is the largest salt marsh in Maine. It is best explored by canoe, and both guided and self-guided tours are available. The marsh rivers are generally placid, so it is fairly easy paddling. Bring your camera, as you never know what surprises await you in the marsh: egrets or herons fishing for food, a muskrat swimming along, or the sight of schools of fish. Foxes, rabbits, raccoons, and other animals make their homes in the tall marsh grass, or come here to hunt. Scarborough Marsh has a nature center with slide shows and exhibits. Restrooms are available. Bug spray is always recommended for outdoor activities in Maine, but if you visit the marsh in August, the greenhead flies can be fierce, so definitely apply repellent before heading out to explore. The Marsh is open for canoe rentals from Memorial Day to Labor Day. For more information, call (207) 883-5100.

With any nature reserve, it is always important that you take care with the plant and wildlife found there. In general, picking flowers or taking any vegetation is forbidden, and since these areas are home to many birds and animals, take care not to disturb nests or dens or frighten the animals, if sighted. The old adage "Take only pictures, leave only footprints," is a wise one to follow.

Route 9 now joins with Route 1 North. Continue on Routes 1 and 9 North until the junction of Route 207 East on your right. Route 207 leads you to **Scarborough Beach Park, Western Beach, Ferry Beach,** and **Prouts Neck.** You will first come to **Scarborough Beach Park,** which is owned by the state. It is a beach with more than one personality. There is a fine swimming beach, with restrooms and picnic tables, and the entire setting is good for little ones. It also has a wild side, with dunes, breaking surf, and marshes. Go for the swimming or to capture its other moods. There is a fee for the park.

Next are **Ferry Beach** and **Western Beach,** which are small, sandy beaches. Ferry Beach has no lifeguards and limited free parking. Western Beach, opposite Ferry Beach, is privately owned, but occasional public use is allowed.

Continue southeast on Route 207 to the beautiful point of land called **Prouts Neck.** Prouts Neck is largely private. It is where the artist Winslow Homer painted many of his famous seascapes. Be sure to take the **Cliff Walk** for some fantastic ocean views; it is one of the few public access points. It is an easy walk, largely level but with a few rocky areas. You might want to stop in at the **Winslow Homer Studio,** which captures the look of the famed artist's work area. Parking is limited, so arrive early.

In the art world, Winslow Homer is considered perhaps this country's greatest nineteenth-century painter. Although he began his career as a water colorist and Civil War illustrator, he is known for his oil paintings of the rugged coast of Maine. Homer's brush perfectly captured the crashing surf and heaving waves of violent storms, the bravery of fishermen battling the elements, and the character of the people who scraped to make a living along this rocky, storm-tossed coast. In Homer's work, you will see fishermen struggling against the waves in a small boat, women almost blown off their feet by the wind, clusters of people huddled against the crashing of the waves on the rocks, dramatic sea rescues, and time and again, depictions of the ocean's terrifying power.

Homer lived by the sea for more than twenty years in a tiny cottage in the fishing village of Prout's Neck. He found this remote, rural spot an ideal place to paint, and created many of his greatest works here. Often he sat sketching right down on the rocks, even when the wind was blowing and 30- and 40-foot waves were pounding the shore. The Homer family has left his cottage studio exactly as it was when he painted his last canvas in 1909. A visit gives not only a glimpse into the artist's life, but a sense of his soul. To see some of his paintings, visit the Portland Museum of Art, which now owns the studio. (See the chapter on Portland, page 101.) Studio hours had not been set at the time of this writing, but you can call the museum at (207) 775-6148 for information.

Continue northeast along the coast on Route 207 to the junction of Route 77. Go right on Route 77 to yet another beach, **Higgins Beach.** Higgins Beach, with its fine sands, is one of the more popular beaches in the area, although it has no restrooms or facilities. There is no fee to use the beach but parking is limited to local businesses who sometimes open a lot and charge a fee. Do not park on the street, as you will be ticketed.

For the next attraction, you will need to reverse direction. Follow Routes 77 and 207 south and back to Route 1. Head south on Route 1 just a short distance to visit **Lenny,** the world's only life-size chocolate moose! That is right, Lenny is 1,700 pounds of milk chocolate. It is no exaggeration to say he is the sweetest moose in Maine! He is big, too, with a full rack of antlers and standing a life-size 6 feet tall. Lenny has been featured on CNN, *Good Morning America,* and in *Yankee Magazine.* You can visit Lenny in his "natural habitat" at **Len Libby Handmade Candies** at 419 U.S. Route 1. Len Libby's has been making candy since 1962 and is run by Fern Hammond, Maine's only Master Confectioner Emeritus. At Len Libby, you can see a video of how Lenny was made, and also enjoy taffy, fudge, lots of other candies, and ice cream. Len Libby's is open year-round, seven days a week. Call (207) 883-4897 or visit **www.lenlibby.com** for more information.

If all that candy has given your children energy to burn, there are lots of ways to do it.

Beech Ridge Speedway is a NASCAR racetrack and one of New England's premier short-track speedways. The track offers five divisions of track action, including a pro series, which features the fastest cars in Maine and is part of the NASCAR Racing Series; a Sport Series, which features some of the most competitive drivers in the nation; and the Wildcats.

In the Sport Series, younger drivers polish their skills while racing at speeds of 80 miles per hour. The Wildcats category is among the most popular, as these are amateur drivers racing street-style cars in non-stop action events. Expect plenty of squealing tires and spinning cars! Two other popular series are the Truck Series and the Lightning Bugs. In the Truck Series, full-size trucks race for the prize. Lightning Bugs is an entry-level division featuring compact cars. Kids will love the blinking lights and colorful antics of these "bugs." Saturday nights are NASCAR nights, and on Friday nights, there is Go-Kart Racing, with divisions for all ages, including kids age six and up. If there is a speedster in your family, Beech Ridge may be the place to turn him or her loose. Kids twelve and under enter free at Beech Ridge Speedway. The season runs from April to September. Call (207) 885-5800 for race times, fees, and additional information, or visit **www.beechridge.com**. Beech Ridge Speedway is at 70 Holmes Road. From Route 1, take the Interstate 95 Connector, but turn right onto Payne Road instead of I-95. From Payne Road, go left onto Holmes Road and Beech Ridge Speedway is on your left.

Scarborough Downs is a different kind of racing, harking back several centuries. Scarborough Downs is Maine's premier harness racing track, with thoroughbred trotters and pacers pulling sulky carts around the track at top speed. Children are not permitted in betting areas, but Scarborough Downs is known for its restaurant, which gives a full view of the track. Many families come to dine and watch the horses compete in this timeless sport. If you are looking for something different, Scarborough Downs may be a good choice. Call (207) 883-4331 for more information. Scarborough Downs is easily reached from Route 1; just turn left onto Scarborough Downs Road.

If your kids feel "the need for speed" then try **Maine Indoor Karting** at 23 Washington Avenue. Children experience the thrill of real formula go-kart racing in a controlled environment. There is carting for teens age sixteen years old and up (must show a valid driver's license or take Maine Indoor Karting's safety class), and carting for children ages eight to fifteen, who must be at least 50 inches tall. These children must also take an education and licensing class. There is a fee for all safety and instruction classes. At this writing, it was $20. Due to the popularity of the classes, you are urged to sign up for classes a day in advance.

The track is 1,200 feet long and 25 feet wide with "white-knuckle turns and exhilarating straightaways." A computerized timing system gives racers lap times and overall results. As noted before, reservations for racing and safety classes are required. Maine Indoor Karting runs year-round and is just off Route 1 at 23 Washington Road. From Route 1 North, turn right onto Lincoln Street, then left onto Washington Road. Call 1-888-246-5278 or visit **www.maine indoorkarting.com**.

🪶 Storms

Most Southern Maine beaches are fine for family swimming. However, storms can change that picture—even storms offshore. Before swimming, check with lifeguards about ocean conditions. If there are no lifeguards, ask the locals about any risks and stay close to shore. Rip currents and under-tows can appear without any easily visible signs. Locals will know which areas are prone to them and when.

Obviously, no one should swim during storm conditions, and most public or lifeguarded beaches will be posted or closed if an offshore storm is kicking up dangerous surf. But even semi-rough surf can put a child or less-experienced swimmer at risk. Good surf offers great boogie boarding and many kids are lured to go out further and further to catch a bigger wave and get a longer ride. If the surf is rough, be in the water with them, and set limits on how far out they can go—don't let them get over their heads. The next wave could be more powerful than those previous and create a situation they cannot handle.

Similarly, it is never wise to turn your back on the ocean—even when knee deep at water's edge. The old tale about waves coming in sets of threes does not always hold true. You can have a good set of waves at a fairly typical size, then have a "rogue" that is much bigger than the rest. If you are not watching, you or your child can be knocked down. Too often people get talking or playing at the ocean's edge and forget the power of the water behind them.

◢ Rip Current Safety

Rip currents, or as they are commonly called, rip tides, do occur along the southern Maine seacoast. (Rip tide is actually a misnomer, as the phenomenon has nothing to do with tidal action.) A rip current is a powerful current of water that flows away from the shore. It can occur at any beach with breaking waves. Every year folks are caught in these dangerous currents, sometimes with tragic results.

Knowing what to look for and how to act if you become caught in one can save your life. You can spot a rip current by looking for any of the following clues:

• A channel of choppy, churning water.
• An area where the water color is noticeably different.
• A line of foam, seaweed, or debris moving steadily seaward.
• A break in the incoming wave pattern.

If you notice any of these signs, stay out of the ocean until the rip current passes. If you get caught in a rip current, try to remember these safety tips:

- Stay calm to conserve energy and think clearly.
- Never fight the current—it will only exhaust you.
- Try to swim out of the current in a direction parallel to the shore.
- When out of the current, swim at an angle away from the current toward the shore.
- If you cannot swim out of the current, calmly float or tread water until the current passes.
- If you are still unable to reach shore, call attention to yourself by yelling and waving your hands. NOTE: Call for help right away if you feel you do not have the ability to swim out of the current or tread water for any length of time.

Rip currents are a good reason to avoid swimming at beaches without lifeguards. If you are at a beach without a lifeguard, it is best to stay in shallower water, and definitely to keep children in the shallows.

🐟 Salt Marshes: Nature's Nursery

Salt marshes and estuaries are the transition areas between the ocean and the land. The salt marsh is the flat grassland surrounding the estuary—the area where fresh water from the land mixes with salt water from the ocean. This blend of environments makes salt marshes unique, and rich in plant and animal life. Though these are vital wild areas, they often have been misunderstood. In the past, most people viewed salt marshes as smelly, buggy places with lots of mud. Upon closer look, the true beauty and importance of the marshes has been revealed.

The heartbeat of the salt marsh is the tide. The changing waters flush the salt marsh each day. Any waste products from naturally decaying materials are carried away with the outgoing tide. The marsh's abundant bacteria also plays a role. As the many plants of the salt marsh decay and die, bacteria break them down into particle form. The tide then mixes these particles and spreads this rich salt marsh "soup" all over the marsh.

This particle mixture is nourishing food for many animals. Microscopic plants and algae feed on this "soup" and they, in turn, are eaten by filter-feeders such as shellfish. The shellfish are then eaten by larger birds and animals—gulls, raccoons, muskrats, and others. And so, the wonderfully complex food web goes on.

Salt marshes are nurseries for many species of fish and shellfish. They serve a key function in the natural food chain, and their bounty is critical to the livelihood of the commercial fishing industry.

Salt marshes play an important role in flood control and protect coastal homes from storm damage. They act as natural buffers against rising tides, and absorb excess water like sponges. Salt marshes are also natural pollution filters and help cleanse our underground water supplies.

Vital as these areas are, the greatest contribution of the salt marsh may be its distinctive beauty. The wind on the water, a heron poised by a tidal pool, the bronze beauty of the waves of grass, and the cry of a hawk wheeling above—these are the essence of a salt marsh.

Author's note: Coastal property is in great demand for development purposes. Because of this, there is increasing pressure to fill or drain salt marshes for building purposes. Key federal legislation already has been weakened and wetlands throughout the country are once again in jeopardy. As you visit reserves such as Scarborough Marsh, consider their beauty and the vital role they play in the health of our coastal ecosystems, the viability of our food supply, and as protective storm barriers. Please think about taking steps to protect wetlands, salt marsh or otherwise, in your own home communities. Talk to your local conservation commissions and conservation agencies such as Audubon and The Nature Conservancy. Write to your legislators. Public input does make a difference, and preserving these vital resources is important for future generations and the health of our planet.

Biddeford Highlights at a Glance

• Beach Avenue
• Hills Beach
• Fortune's Rocks Beach

- Biddeford Pool
- Rotary Park Beach
- East Point Sanctuary
- Brush Brook Stables: (207) 284-7721
- Wood Island Light
- La Kermesse Franco-Americaine Festival: (207) 282-2894

Saco Highlights at a Glance

- Camp Ellis
- Bay View Beach
- Kinney Shores
- Ferry Beach State Park
- Saco Heath
- Funtown/Splashtown: (207) 284-5139
- Aquaboggan Water Park: (207) 282-3112
- Biddeford/Saco Chamber of Commerce: (207) 282-1567

Old Orchard Beach Highlights at a Glance

- Old Orchard Beach
- Old Orchard Beach Pier
- Palace Playland: (207) 934-2001
- Pirates Cove Adventure Golf: (207) 934-5086
- Old Orchard Beach Town Square Concerts
- Annual Car Show
- Christmas Events
- Old Orchard Beach Chamber of Commerce: (207) 934-2500

- Elk Farm
- Scarborough River Wildlife Preserve and Bird Sanctuary: (207) 883-8427
- Scarborough Marsh Nature Center: (207) 883-5100
- Scarborough Beach State Park
- Ferry Beach and Western Beach
- Prouts Neck and the Winslow Homer Studio
- Higgins Beach
- Lenny, the giant chocolate moose, Len Libby Handmade Candies: (207) 883-4897
- Beech Ridge Speedway: (207) 885-5800
- Scarborough Downs: (207) 883-4331
- Maine Indoor Karting: (888) 246-5278

This is the start of Maine's rockier coast, yet beautiful beaches are still to be found. Visit Two Lights State Park and the famous Portland Head Light. Sail out to one of the harbor's many islands by motorized craft, sailboat, or an historic sailing vessel such as a schooner. Downtown, visit the Children's Museum of Maine, Portland Observatory, or Maine Narrow Gauge Railroad Museum. Stroll the Old Port with its incredible shops and restaurants, and see a working waterfront. Come evening, take in a Sea Dogs baseball game and enjoy all the fun and excitement of minor league ball.

Route 1 now brings you right into **Portland.** Portland is Maine's largest city and its cultural hub. If you want all an urban environment has to offer, but also want to explore the southern coast, then Portland is a great base. Your first stop in Portland should be one of the city's **visitor information centers.** The city produces an excellent full-color brochure, which includes a detailed map, extensive restaurant and accommodation listings, locations of restrooms and parking garages, some coupons, and much more. The main visitor information center is located downtown at 245 Commercial Street. As you come into the Portland city exits, take the exit for the waterfront, as Commercial Street is the waterfront street. At the end of the bridge, bear right onto Commercial Street. The visitor center is marked. This visitor center is open Mondays through Fridays, 8:00 A.M. to 5:00 P.M., and Saturdays and holidays, 10:00 A.M. to 5:00 P.M., from mid-May to mid-October. During the off-season, from mid-October through mid-May, the hours are Mondays through Fridays, 8:00 A.M. to 5:00 P.M., and Saturdays and holidays, 10:00 A.M. to 3:00 P.M. Call (207) 772-5800 for more information. Visitor centers also are located at the Portland Jetport and at the Cruise Ship Terminal (see previous directions for Commercial Street), in season.

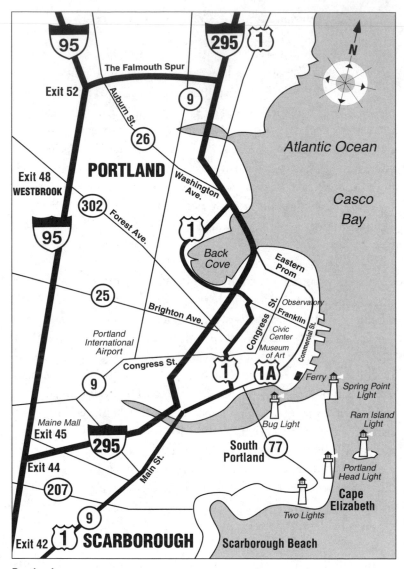

Portland

Portland is packed with family fun: visiting famous lighthouses, cruising to its harbor islands, splashing about with the Downeast Duck Tours, playing at the Children's Museum, taking a train ride, and much more. *Map by Denise Brown of Ad-Cetera Graphics.*

See sidebar on directions in downtown Portland, page 105.

Parking in the city is at metered spaces, parking lots, or parking garages. Meters are operational Monday through Saturday from 9:00 A.M. to 6:00 P.M., except on holidays. Parking garage prices vary, and again, are shown on the visitor center brochure map. In winter, parking may be restricted due to snow removal. Call (207) 879-0300 for winter parking information.

Portland is Maine's largest city, with a population of 62,500. Nearly a quarter of the state's total population lives within the greater Portland area. Portland is a coastal city, wrapped around a deep-water harbor. Shipping, shipbuilding, fishing, lobstering, trade, ferry services—all the activities of a working waterfront drive a good part of Portland's economy. Indeed, the spirit of the sea is woven throughout Portland's culture, history, architecture, and entertainment offerings.

Portland was first settled in 1633. Although the area was blessed with many natural resources, some early arrivals may have wondered if the city would ever truly take hold. Portland burned to the ground not once, but four times. In 1866, the city rose from the ashes for the last time, and adopted the mythical bird, the phoenix, as its totem. According to legend, the phoenix also rises from the ashes after being consumed by flame. Much of Portland's architecture is mid-nineteenth century, reflecting that last, determined reconstruction.

Portland faces Casco Bay, a waterway rich in islands, historic forts, and lighthouses. One could easily spend a week exploring Portland and the Bay's islands and historic sites. One of the first stops would have to be the **Old Port,** with its cobblestone streets, shops, restaurants, waterfront parks, and working waterfront. (The Old Port is bound by Commercial Street on the waterfront side; see previous directions.) A range of cruise boats offers narrated tours of the Bay; there are naturalist cruises promising views of seals and seabirds, lighthouse exploration tours, and lobster bake cruises. You can take a cruise on motorized craft, schooners, or sailboats. You can rent a sailboat, paddle boats, or a kayak for a more personal exploration of the harbor.

Within Casco Bay are the fabled **Calendar Islands**—365 is the claimed number, hence the name, but purists state that 222 is the actual count. They can be reached by ferry from Portland. Every island is different, but they all have one thing in common—a slower pace and closer harmony with sea and sky. Many of the islands offer great trails for hiking or biking, rocky shores to explore, or small, sandy beaches. Bring a picnic lunch and spend the day. Some of the islands, such as **Peaks, Diamond Cove,** and **Long Island,** have dining facilities and provide a fantastic view of Portland while you enjoy your dinner. A few have overnight accommodations, such as **Great Chebeague Island** with its famed Chebeague Island Inn. Great Chebeague or the "Island of Many Springs" also has beaches, sailing, tennis, and golf. It is also good for hiking and picnicking. Grab a picnic lunch at the Island Market and head for adventure! **Peaks Island** is a great trip for kids, as there are hourly departures in summer (through Casco Bay Lines, the islands' main ferry service), lots of places to hike and bike, beaches, and tidepooling. The island has restaurants and shops, and an ice cream parlor. You can rent bikes on the island or bring yours aboard the ferry. Contact the Maine Tourism Association at (207) 439-1319 or Casco Bay Lines (more below) for more information.

To visit the islands for a few hours or a day, catch a ferry from **Casco Bay Lines,** located on Commercial Street at the foot of Franklin Street in the Old Port. The cruise line is plainly marked and will be on your right as you head east on Commercial Street. For reservations, and a current schedule, visit **www.cascobaylines .com,** or call (207) 774-7871. Ferry service is year-round, and Casco Bay Lines offers a wide range of seasonal cruises, featuring the islands, naturalist trips, lighthouses, lobster bakes, and more. Other cruise options include **Bay View Cruises** at 184 Commercial Street, which offers beverage and snack service on board, and can provide a lobster bake on request, and **Classic Bay Cruises,** with offices at 488 Fessenden Street, which allows you to explore the Bay from the deck of a classic Chris Craft Constellation. For reservations and more information on Bay View Cruises, call (207) 761-0496 or visit www.bayviewcruiseme.com. For more information or reservations for Classic Bay Cruises, call (207) 671-2210 or visit www.classic baycruises.com.

Reservations for all of the cruises mentioned in this section are strongly suggested, and in many cases, may be required, so call ahead to avoid disappointment.

Other unique tours include **Lucky Catch Cruises** at 170 Commercial Street, which allow you to experience lobstering firsthand. Aprons, boots, and gloves are supplied for those hardy enough to haul traps, or you can sit back and watch the crew work. Call (207) 761-0941 or visit **www.luckycatch.com** for more information. **Palawan Sailing** at the Long Wharf on Commercial Street takes you among the islands of Casco Bay on a vintage 58-foot ocean racing sailboat. Call (207) 773-2163 or visit **www.sailpalawan.com**. The **Portland Schooner Company** at the Maine State Pier on Commercial Street offers sailboats for charter and tours. If you want to "catch a fair wind," call (207) 766-2500 or visit **www .portlandschooner.com** for more details. **Ophelia's Odyssey** at 231 Front Street gives you the choice of sailing on the schooner *Ophelia's Dream* or the Friendship Sloop *Ophelia's Odyssey* while exploring the harbor. Friendship sloops are distinctive sailing vessels built in Friendship, Maine, since the 1880s. They are graceful boats, known for their clipper-style bow, generous-sized cockpit, a boom as long as the hull, and, as one sailor put it, "a gorgeous load of sail." Call (207) 590-3145 for more information. The **Old Port Mariner Fleet** at the Long Wharf on Commercial Street offers whale-watching, scenic, and dinner cruises. To set sail with them, call (207) 775-0727.

While exploring the waterfront, be sure to enjoy some classic Maine seafood from some of Portland's famous restaurants. One of the "must- experience" places is **DiMillo's Floating Restaurant** on the Long Wharf in the Old Port. As you head east on Commercial Street, DiMillo's is on your right, just before the Custom House Wharf and berth for Casco Bay Lines. You cannot miss this landmark restaurant. DiMillo's has been a Maine dining experience since 1980. The restaurant is actually a converted car ferry that once ran from New Castle, Delaware, to Jamestown, Rhode Island. In 1980, it was sold to the DeMillo family and converted to one of the largest floating restaurants in America. Known for its fabulous waterfront views, DiMillo's is an excellent choice for lobster, seafood, and chowder. Call (207) 772-2216 for reservations and more information. A children's menu is available.

Gilbert's Chowder House, at (207) 871-5632, also in the Old Port at 92 Commercial Street, is another popular seafood spot with reasonable prices. Gilbert's is known for their award-winning chowder, voted the "Best in Maine" by the *Maine Sunday Telegram*. You can dine inside or outdoors on the patio. The **Portland Lobster Company** at 180 Commercial Street is a more casual dining experience, and allows you to eat in or take out. They specialize in steamed lobster, lobster stew, clam cakes, fish and chips, fried scallops, steamed mussels, and more. The Lobster Company invites you to "get crackin'" and join them on the deck in the Old Port. Call (207) 775-2112 for reservations.

Many seafood choices, especially lobster and clams, can be high in price. Prices are often "market value" and not listed on the menu, so you will be wise to ask before ordering. Chowders, fish and chips, and other seafood fare can be much lower in price. Most restaurants also offer non-seafood items, such as burgers or sandwiches in casual eateries, or chicken, pasta, or beef choices in fine-dining establishments. If you can afford the cost, it will certainly be a tasty experience for the family to enjoy a Maine lobster or basket of fried clams or steamers while here. If you wonder about your children's appetite for lobster or clams, or wish to economize, consider sharing an order.

If seafood is not your cup of tea, Portland offers a truly eclectic dining selection. Italian, Indian, Vietnamese, Thai, Japanese, Chinese, Mexican, steakhouses, and much more can be found here. There are also plenty of family-style restaurants, take-out places, and sub shops. For a complete dining guide, stop in at the Conventions and Visitors Bureau of Greater Portland at 245 Commercial Street in the Old Port. One non-seafood item that Portland is known for is its **Amatos** sandwiches, found at the restaurant by the same name. An Amatos is a classic Italian sandwich. It is a unique taste of Maine with an Italian twist! Amatos also offers pizza, pasta, calzones, and salads. Younger children may not care for the strong Italian flavoring, but would certainly enjoy an Amatos pizza. Look for Amatos at 71 India Street in the Old Port or call (207) 773-1682 for more information.

No one can come to Portland without seeing the area's famous lighthouses. The signature lighthouse is **Portland Head Light,** one of the most photographed and painted lighthouses in the country. Portland Head Light was commissioned in 1792 by President George Washington, and stands in Fort Williams Park in Cape Elizabeth. Its beacon still shines from an 80-foot tower made of white fieldstone and brick at the entrance to Portland Harbor. The red-roofed keeper's cottage is now home to a small museum that chronicles the history of Portland Head Light and

Portland Head Light and its rocky coast. *Photo by Marcia Peverly.*

the fort, which was a military outpost for coastal defense. The museum is open daily, June to October, and weekends only in April, May, November, and December. Portland Head Light is part of **Fort Williams Town Park,** located off Shore Road in Cape Elizabeth, about 8 miles south of Portland. The park is open from sunrise to sunset daily.

To reach Portland Head Light, Fort Williams State Park, Two Lights State Park (Two Lights actually comes first), Spring Point Ledge Light, Spring Point Museum, and the Bug Light from Portland's waterfront area, go up one street from Commercial Street. If you are at the east end of Commercial, look for Fore Street. If you are at the west end of Commercial, look for Danforth Street. Head west on Fore Street to Danforth Street and watch for signs for Route 77 and South Portland. Cross the bridge into South Portland and head south on Route 77. Route 77 will loop around the headland, bringing you first to Two Lights. Watch closely for Two Lights Road on your left. There is a sign, but it can be missed.

Two Lights State Park is so-called because it is home to two lighthouses: Cape Elizabeth West and Cape Elizabeth Light. Cape Elizabeth Light was originally built in 1828, but was then replaced in 1874. Its 67-foot, conical, white cast-iron tower is still an important navigation aid, and its light is considered the most powerful in New England. It sits at the entrance to Casco Bay. Cape Elizabeth West is the sister lighthouse to Cape Elizabeth Light. It was also built in 1828 and replaced in 1874. The 27-foot cast-iron tower was deactivated in 1928 and is now privately owned.

Both **Two Lights State Park** and the earlier-mentioned **Fort Williams Town Park** are great places to explore, picnic, and take photos. In addition to impressive views of the lighthouses, they offer splendid views of the harbor and bay. Fort Williams Town Park covers 90 acres. Explore the ruins of the fort, play tennis, fly a kite (great breezes here), and dip your toes in the surf. (Be careful, though. This is not a swimming area as there is a strong undertow.) At Two Lights, enjoy the picturesque walkway that wraps around the peninsula. Call (207) 799-5871 for more information about Two Lights State Park, and (207) 799-7652 for more information on Fort Williams.

To continue on to Portland Head Light, go back out Two Lights Road, then go right onto Route 77 North, then right again onto Shore Road. As mentioned earlier, Portland Head Light is in Fort Williams State Park and is off Shore Road, on your right.

Ram Island Ledge Light is a 70-foot, gray granite, conical tower at the north side of Portland Harbor. Built in 1905, it is still an active navigational aid. The lighthouse is accessible only by boat and not open to the public. Still, it is worth noting, as it is part of the area's heritage and easily visible in the harbor.

To reach the next lighthouse, take Shore Road east. From Shore Road, go right onto Preble Street east to Fort Road to reach Spring Point Ledge Light. **Spring Point Ledge Light** marks the dangerous ledge on the west side of the main shipping channel into Portland Harbor. Many vessels ran aground here until a group of steamship companies convinced the government to locate a lighthouse on the ledge in 1891. A series of setbacks delayed construction until 1897. The lighthouse is short and round and made of brick. It includes four levels, including a keeper's office, watchroom, and two levels for living quarters. The light was electrified and automated in 1934. In 1951, the 900-foot breakwater was constructed, joining the lighthouse with the mainland.

Spring Point Ledge Light is also easily accessible. You can walk right out to the light, and on your return visit the **Portland Harbor Museum** (locally called the **Spring Point Museum**) in the adjacent Southern Maine Technical College campus. The museum contains lighthouse and maritime exhibits, which change annually. Past themes have included shipwrecks and lighthouse lore. One permanent display includes sections of the clipper ship *Snow Squall.* Built for speed, clipper ships came into their own in the early to mid-1880s. They were the work horses of the China Trade, sailing regularly from harbors along the eastern coast of the United States to bring exotic goods from the Far East. Many clipper ships were built in Maine, and were a familiar site in her harbors during that period.

The museum is open daily 10:00 A.M. to 4:00 P.M. from June to September. Hours in the spring and fall can vary, so call (207) 799-6337 or visit www.portlandharbormuseum.org.

Fort Preble is located on the Southern Maine Technical College campus as well. Built in 1808, this fort was part of the area's defense from the War of 1812 through World War II. Take a moment to stroll around and sample this part of Maine's history.

Portland Breakwater "Bug" Light is located in South Portland on the west side of Portland Harbor's main channel. Built in 1855 and deactivated in 1942, the light is a sturdy, stubby tower sitting atop an octagonal stone pier. The tower stands only 20 feet tall and is made of cast iron. The grounds are open to the public, and you may walk the breakwater directly out to the lighthouse to view it up close. The grounds include a shoreline walkway and playing field. The "Bug" Light (so-called because it looks like a short, squat bug) offers wonderful views and is a great way to get a close-up look at a lighthouse. To reach the "Bug" Light from Spring Point Ledge Light, take Pickett Road to Breakwater Road to Madison Road. The lighthouse is at the end of Madison.

Halfway Rock Light is located halfway between Portland Head Light and Seguin Light in Georgetown. This 77-foot tower, made of granite, can be seen from either Fort Williams Park in Cape Elizabeth or from the end of Route 24 at Bailey Island in Harpswell.

Portland is a city blessed with **abundant parks and trails,** both within city limits and nearby. One of the most popular trails is along **Back Cove,** where a scenic path runs beside tidal flats and Baxter Boulevard, one of the city's main thoroughfares. This is a good stretch for biking, jogging, rollerblading, or just taking in the scenery, but the entire walk may be too long for younger children. To walk all the way down and all the way back is nearly 6 miles. The trail connects Back Cove to East End Beach at the Eastern Promenade (see next set of directions). Or, take a walk along the **Eastern Promenade.** The Eastern Promenade covers 68 acres and includes ball fields, tennis courts, playgrounds, and panoramic views of Casco Bay. Head east on Commercial Street, which is also Route 1A. Turn left onto Frankline Street, which is also Route 1A. Take your first right onto Fore Street. Fore Street connects to the Eastern Promenade. By contrast, the **Western Promenade** takes you through one of the country's best-preserved Victorian residential districts, with stunning views of the water and historic homes. To reach the Western Promenade, go west on Commercial Street and turn right onto High Street. From High Street, turn left onto Danforth Street. Watch for the Western Promenade on your right.

Deering Oaks Park is lush with flower gardens and children will enjoy the duck pond. Its 51 acres also include a snack bar, tennis courts, basketball courts, ball fields, and playgrounds. If you visit in winter, the park is a popular ice skating spot. Deering Oaks Park is between Deering Avenue, Forest Avenue, and Park Avenue; take Exit 6A off Route 295, the by-pass belt around Portland. **Baxter Woods** is a touch of wildness in the heart of the city. Located in residential Portland, between Forest and Stevens Avenues, it is a woodland park and bird sanctuary. Take Exit 6B off of Route 295, the by-pass belt around Portland. **Fore River Sanctuary** is 2.5-mile system of trails along the Fore River. Take the Congress Street exit, exit 5, off Route 295.

If you want a **guided tour of the city,** options abound. **Mainely Tours & Gifts Trolley Line** departs from their Old Port Gift Shop at 163 Commercial Street and takes you on a ninety-minute trolley ride through the city. History, architecture, natural areas, and attractions are highlighted. Call (207) 774-0808 for tickets or for more information, or visit **www.mainelytours.com. Working Waterfront Tours** at 73 Vesper Street takes a nontraditional approach, leading you on an hour-long walking tour of Portland's bustling harbor. Lobstering, fishing, and other marine-related businesses are showcased as you and your guide explore the wharves and walkways of the waterfront. For a glimpse of Portland's seafaring heart, this is a unique journey. Call (207) 415-0765 for tickets or more information, or visit **www.marinerfleet.com.** Working

Waterfront Tours is near the Eastern Promenade in the waterfront district.

Children will especially enjoy the **Downeast Duck Adventure.** These amphibious tours of Portland concentrate on the historical and scenic aspects of the harbor. Climb aboard the forty-nine-passenger *Eider* for a lot of fun with some education thrown in. You will learn about Revolutionary War battles, ride to the top of the Promenade and get a panoramic view of the Calendar Islands, then splash back into Casco Bay to view the working waterfront, lighthouses, and basking seals. This is Portland's (and Maine's) only amphibious touring vessel and space books up quickly in summer. Tours depart daily at 10:00 A.M., noon, 2:00 P.M., and 4:00 P.M. Tours average about 80 minutes. You can purchase tickets at Casco Variety (also known as the "Quack Shack") at 94 Commercial Street, or by calling (207) 774-DUCK (3825). Visit www.downeastduck.com for more information.

Portland is filled with **historic sites and museums.** These are perfect for a rainy day. One of the most incredible sites is the **Victoria Mansion** at 109 Danforth Street. Children will be intrigued by this glimpse into a lavish lifestyle of another time, as the mansion could easily be home to a prince or a princess. The Victoria Mansion was built before the Civil War as the summer home of New Orleans hotelier Ruggles S. Morse. Inside, the mansion is richly decorated with fresco painting, stained glass, statuary, carvings, chandeliers, and many of the original ornate furnishings. It is the last surviving commission of famed New York designer Gustave Herter.

The Victoria Mansion is open May through October, Tuesday through Saturday, 10:00 A.M. to 4:00 P.M., and Sundays 1:00 P.M. to 5:00 P.M. It is closed Mondays, July 4, and Labor Day. Special Christmas hours are held in December. For more information, call (207) 772-4841. Danforth Street is not far from the Old Port district.

Less lavish, but worth paying a visit to, is the **Wadsworth-Longfellow House** at 485 Congress Street, the childhood home of esteemed American poet Henry Wadsworth Longfellow, who was born in Portland. Children may no longer memorize "Hiawatha" in school, but nearly everyone has a favorite Longfellow poem or knows of one. Built in the 1850s, the house is one of the oldest brick structures on Portland's peninsula. It has been faithfully restored and decorated with original furnishings and family memorabilia. You can even see where Henry wrote on the walls as a child! The Longfellow House is located in the heart of the downtown, and is part of the Maine Historical Society's 1-acre campus. The Longfellow House is open May to October, Mondays and Saturdays 10:00 A.M. to 4:00 P.M., and Sundays noon to 4:00 P.M. Weekend and holiday hours are available in November and December. For more information, call (207) 774-1822 or visit **www.maine history.org**. Longfellow's statue can be seen in Longfellow Square, at the corner of State and Congress streets. To reach the Longfellow House, take Exit 5 off Route 295, then follow the signs for Route 22 East and downtown.

Another rainy day favorite is the **Portland Museum of Art**, which offers not only an astounding collection of paintings, sculpture, furniture, and other art forms, but also hands-on arts activities for children. Have lunch in the museum café, browse the gift shop, listen to the musical performances frequently held in the gallery, and let your creativity run wild! The Portland Museum of Art is found at Seven Congress Square, also in the heart of the downtown. The museum generally is open seven days, but there is some fluctuation with hours due to seasons and special events, so your best bet is to visit the web site at **www.portlandmuseumofart .org**, or call (207) 775-6148 when you visit. See the directions for the Longfellow House.

Over at 157 Spring Street, stop by the **Portland Fire Museum** at 157 Spring Street, which depicts the history of firefighting in Portland and houses a wealth of firefighting memorabilia. Given the fact that the city suffered four major conflagrations in its early years, there are some pretty incredible tales to tell. The Portland Fire Museum is also near the Old Port.

The **Children's Museum of Maine** offers a wide range of indoor interactive exhibits and programs for families, including L. L. Bear's

Discovery Woods, the Dress-Up Theatre, Toddler Park, and Ship Ahoy! Children can immerse themselves in the Maine woods at Discovery Woods, where they can dam a stream, build a shelter, climb Mt. Kid-ta-din, and much more. (Yes, it's all indoors.) The Dress-Up Theatre lets kids create and stage their own play, complete with costumes, props, and stage. On Ship Ahoy! they can set sail for far ports on their own "tall ship for small people." There are also planetarium shows and the amazing Camera Obscura, a visual wonder that gives you the best view of Portland from inside a room with no windows. You will have to try it yourself to see how it works. "Discover the power of play," as the museum says, at 142 Free Street in downtown Portland, right next to the Museum of Art. During the summer, the museum is open Monday through Saturday 10:00 A.M. to 5:00 P.M. and Sundays noon to 5:00 P.M. During the fall, winter, and spring, the hours are Tuesday through Saturday, 10:00 A.M. to 5:00 P.M., and Sundays noon to 5:00 P.M. The first Friday of every month, the museum is open free of admission from 5:00 P.M. to 8:00 P.M. School vacation weeks have special hours, so call ahead. For more information, call (207) 828-1234 or visit **www.kitetails.com**. See the directions for the Longfellow House.

The **Maine Narrow Gauge Railroad Museum,** down at 58 Fore Street, is fun rain or shine. The whistle blows and it is all aboard for a 3-mile ride in an historic train along Casco Bay. Rides average about 30 minutes. The museum itself is home to classic 2-foot-gauge locomotives and railroad cars, including coaches, open cars, and a caboose. Model-T trucks and antique machine tools are also featured. Trains run daily mid-May to mid-October, and special steam trains run on holiday weekends (popular Santa trains run in late November and December). The train museum is open daily 10:00 A.M. to 4:00 P.M. Call (207) 828-0814 or visit **www.mngrr.org** for more information. The railroad museum is within walking distance of the Eastern Promenade.

Take a trip into space at the **Southworth Planetarium** on the campus of the University of Southern Maine. The planetarium offers a variety of astronomy and laser light shows sure to capture the imagination of any budding astronaut or astronomer. Call (207) 780-4249 for more information. To reach the planetarium, take Exit 6B off Route 295 to Forest Avenue, then go left onto Falmouth Street.

Before leaving Portland, make sure you stop by the **Portland Observatory.** Built in 1807, and looking much like a lighthouse on land, the Observatory is an old maritime signal tower located at the top of Munjoy Hill at 138 Congress Street. The only remaining maritime signal tower in America, it offers spectacular views of Portland and Casco Bay, and shares some of the city's maritime history. The observatory is open daily from 10:00 A.M. to 5:00 P.M. from May through mid-October. For more information, call (207) 774-5561 or visit **www.portlandlandmarks.org.** To visit the observatory, take Exit 7 off Route 295 onto Franklin Street, then go left onto Congress Street and head east.

As you stroll Portland, it is worth noting the **Whaling Wall** on Franklin and Commercial Streets, right next to the Maine State Pier and Casco Bay Lines Terminal. The Whaling Wall, which depicts near-life-size marine life, was done in 1993 by the famed marine artist Wyland, as part of his East Coast Whaling Wall tour, which had him creating whaling walls in significant Eastern coastal cities. The walls are designed to call attention to the beauty and importance of the sea and its creatures. Wyland travels all over the world creating paintings and sculpture that further his mission of protecting the world's oceans.

The **statue of legendary film director John Ford,** a Portland native, stands at the corner of Pleasant and Danforth Streets. Ford was known for his western classics such as *Fort Apache* and *She Wore a Yellow Ribbon,* many of them starring John Wayne.

At the corner of Pleasant and Park Streets stands the Holy Trinity Church, and in its lobby is a **bell cast by Paul Revere.** It is one of the last remaining Revere bells in the state.

If you visit Portland in summer, then you need to spend at least one evening enjoying that **classic American pastime of baseball.** The **Portland Sea Dogs,** an Eastern League AA Affiliate of the

Boston Red Sox, play ball at Hadlock Field at 271 Park Avenue. Tickets are very reasonable, making for an affordable family evening. The AA ball is good, and without the intense pressure and hype of big league games. It is family baseball at its best.

Every inning, some kind of fun activity takes place. Giant beach balls are thrown to the crowd; the Sea Dog mascot, Slugger, races a child around the bases; contestants are chosen to throw plastic lobsters into baskets. There are prizes and raffles, the singing of "Take Me Out to the Ball Game" at the seventh-inning stretch, and all the classic baseball food: popcorn, hotdogs, peanuts, and yes, Cracker Jack! The park is clean and parking is available at a nearby garage. For this summer's schedule, visit **www.seadogs.com**. You can order tickets on-line at this same web address, or call (207) 874-9300. Tickets go fast, so purchase early. To reach the ballfield, take Exit 6A, the Forest Avenue South exit off Route 295. Next, take your first right off Forest Avenue onto State Street, then go right again onto Park Avenue. Bear in mind that there is very little parking right at the ballfield. However, there is ample parking on the street, and in parking lots and garages nearby. Allow time to park.

If winter brings you to Portland, check out the **Portland Pirates Hockey Team,** the American Hockey League Affiliate of the Washington Capitals (NHL). The Pirates play forty home games at the Cumberland County Civic Center on Spring Street, and tickets are very reasonably priced. Similar to the Sea Dogs, Pirates games have good hockey with a family emphasis. To get tickets or more information, visit **www.portlandpirates.com**, or call (207) 828-4665. To reach the civic center, take Exit 7 off Route 295, then turn right onto Middle Street, which will become Spring Street. There is a parking garage at the center.

Events are always underway in Portland, but some deserve special note. In the summer, take in a **concert at Deering Oaks Park.** Every Tuesday evening, enjoy music under the stars. Pack a picnic and grab some blankets or a lawn chair. Thursdays, there are **concerts at the Gazebo in Portland's Fort Allen Park** (off Fore

Street, near the Eastern Promenade), and also the **"Alive at Five"** concerts at 5:00 P.M. in Monument Square. On Mondays, **enjoy outdoor movies in Congress Square.** For this year's schedules, contact the Portland Visitor Center at (207) 772-5800.

June brings the **Old Port Festival,** held at the Old Port Exchange on Exchange Street. The Exchange is packed with crafts and food booths, children's activities, music, and live entertainment. For more information and this year's date, call (207) 772-6828. To reach Exchange Street, take Exit 6A off Route 295 to Congress Street and turn left. Go approximately three blocks, then turn right onto Exchange Street (note that Exchange is a one-way street).

August has two major events, starting with the **Beach to Beacon Race,** a 10-kilometer road race from Crescent Beach State Park to Portland Head Light. It usually attracts more than five thousand runners from around the country and the world. Call (800) 480-6940 for more information.

Next is the **Regatta Harborfest,** a sailboat race in Portland Harbor. Each year, the event benefits a different charity. In addition to the spectacular sight of dozens of sailboats underway, the event features music and food on the Portland Pier and a display of tug boats. Call (207) 761-5815 for information on this year's event.

Come late November through December 31, Portland throws its **Light Up the Holidays** festival, with special parades, decorated historic homes, carolers, fairs, and musical performances. Call (207) 772-6828 for details.

The old year is rung out and the New Year in with **New Year's Portland** on December 31, a non-alcoholic, city-wide celebration featuring music, dance, food, and family entertainment. For information on this year's event, call (207) 772-6828.

⚓ *Directions in Downtown Portland*

Because the city has been rebuilt and revamped several times over its history, and because of its size, it is not possible to give detailed directions here. You are well advised to stop at the Portland visitor centers noted at the start of this chapter for explicit directions and a detailed map. However, some directions are noted here in order to provide general bearings. Many sites are close together, so if you find one, you will be within easy walking distance of others. The Portland chapter started by directing you down to the waterfront, which is one of Portland's activity hubs for commerce as well as tourism. This section is used as a reference many times as we orient you to several other attractions in the general area. The Old Port is fairly easy to walk, there are trolleys, and quite a few places to park, so it is a good base.

In other cases, where attractions are well removed from the Old Port, directions are given from Route 295, the main by-pass artery around Portland. To connect onto Route 295 from Interstate 95, take Exit 44. If you have come into Portland from Route 1 or Route 77, you will also see signs for Route 295 North.

◢ *The Mystique of Lighthouses*

Maine has sixty-five lighthouses along its more than 300-mile coastline. Most are at the ocean's edge, but a few are at the mouths of rivers. Lighthouses were built to warn ships of dangerous shoals, jutting cliffs, partially submerged islands, and other hazards to navigation. They also helped ships find the coast or the harbor entrance in times of storm. Most lighthouses not only shine a beacon, they also sound an audible alarm, either the traditional foghorn or sometimes a clanging bell.

In earlier times, the shining of the beacon and the sounding of an alarm had to be done manually. The lighthouses had "keepers," who usually lived at the lighthouse in some type of cottage. (In a few cases, there were no accommodations and the keeper went back and forth from the mainland to tend the lighthouse.) During winter or storms, keepers could be up all night or even longer making sure the light stayed on and the alarm sounded. They were at risk themselves, as it is not unusual for raging storms along the Maine coast to send waves piling right over the lighthouses.

The tall tower of Portland Head Light. *Photo by Marcia Peverly.*

Since many lighthouses are on islands, being a lighthouse keeper often meant living in semi-isolation. All of the groceries, househould necessities, and medical supplies had to be ferried over. If there were storms, keepers and their families could not get ashore; they had to go without until a crossing was possible. (Many keepers attempted island gardens in summers, but in a lot of cases the soil was too poor or rocky for planting. Some also kept livestock, such as chickens.) Lighthouse keepers also had to deal with medical emergencies themselves. If you were alone and in trouble, there was no one to come to your aid. Being a lighthouse keeper was not for the faint of heart.

It was particularly hard on keepers' wives, who had to deal with long months of solitude, the difficulty of keeping a household together, and the hazards of their husband's work. In winter, keepers and their families were often pretty much housebound. The islands and rocks would be covered with ice and it was too risky to venture outside very often—one slip and you could be off into the surf and drown. Keepers took a chance just making their way to the lighthouse tower. They frequently strung a rope—a lifeline—from house to tower to give them hope of safe passage.

Some keepers had children with them, and while for some it was lonely, many loved the lighthouse life. Celia Thaxter, the nineteenth-century author and artist, grew up on White Island, one of the Isles of Shoals off the Maine Coast. Her father was the keeper there, and Celia loved the freedom and wildness of the islands. She was fascinated by the sea creatures, the booming surf, and wind-carved rocks. She loved the daily procession of boats passing by and the closeness with her family as they hunkered down against winter storms. As she grew up, Celia drew inspiration from the breathless sweep of sky and sea, and although she lived on the mainland for a time during the early years of her marriage, the islands called her back. She returned to island life with her son to live out her days.

Many keepers shared Celia's love for the lighthouse life. Some found it hard to go back to the hustle and bustle of the mainland after living in such quietude. They grew to love the closeness to the sea, the sound of wind, wave, and gull, the chance to see nature in all her fierce glory. Being a lighthouse keeper was almost a calling, and for those who responded, it called to the soul in a way that few other occupations did.

Portland Area Highlights at a Glance

- Old Port
- Calendar Islands
- Casco Bay Lines: (207) 774-7871
- Bay View Cruises: (207) 761-0496
- Classic Bay Cruises: (207) 761-2210
- Lucky Catch Cruises: (207) 761-0941
- Palawan Sailing: (207) 773-2163
- Portland Schooner Company: (207) 766-2500
- Ophelia's Odyssey: (207) 590-3145
- Old Port Mariner Fleet: (207) 775-0727
- DeMillo's Floating Restaurant: (207) 772-2216
- Gilbert's Chowder House: (207) 871-5632
- Portland Maine Lobster Company: (207) 775-2112
- Amatos: (207) 773-1682
- Portland Head Light
- Fort Williams Town Park: (207) 799-7652
- Two Lights State Park: (207) 799-5871
- Ram Island Ledge Light
- Spring Point Ledge Light
- Portland Harbor Museum: (207) 799-6337
- Portland Breakwater "Bug" Light
- Halfway Rock Light
- Back Cove Trail, Eastern Promenade, and Western Promenade
- Deering Oaks Park, Baxter Woods, and Fore River Sanctuary
- Mainely Tours & Gifts Trolley Line: (207) 774-0808
- Working Waterfront Tours: (207) 415-0765
- Downeast Duck Adventure: (207) 774-DUCK (3825)
- Victoria Mansion: (207) 772-4841
- Wadsworth-Longfellow House: (207) 774-1882
- Portland Museum of Art: (207) 775-6148
- Portland Fire Museum: Call visitor center: (207) 772-5800
- Children's Museum of Maine: (207) 828-1234
- Maine Narrow Gauge Railroad Museum: (207) 828-0814

- Southworth Planetarium: (207) 780-4249
- Portland Observatory: (207) 774-5561
- Whaling Wall, John Ford statue, Longfellow statue, and Paul Revere bell
- Portland Sea Dogs AA baseball: (207) 874-9300
- Portland Pirates AHL Hockey: (207) 828-4665
- Concerts at Deering Oaks Park, Fort Allen Park, and Monument Square
- Monday movies in Congress Square
- Old Port Festival: (207) 772-6828
- Beach to Beacon Race: (800) 480-6940
- Regatta Harborfest: (207) 761-5815
- Light Up the Holidays: (207) 772-6828
- New Year's Portland: (207) 772-6828
- Portland Visitors Center: (207) 772-5800

These towns are all known for their scenic coastlines, and families will find a wide range of activities to choose from. A must-see is the world's premier outdoor store, L. L. Bean—open 24 hours a day, 365 days a year. It is tradition to shop there at midnight at least once! Wild beauty abounds in area state parks, with plenty of opportunities for hiking and picnicking. See the ospreys at Wolfe's Neck Woods. Marvel at a unique quirk of nature at the Desert of Maine. Admire Herbie, the giant elm, and the DeLorme Mapping Company's giant globe. Take a boat cruise or spend time exploring the rocky shore.

The communities of Falmouth, Yarmouth, and Freeport, just north of Portland, all offer great opportunities for boat cruises, deep-sea fishing, wonderful ocean views, and even some nice, small beaches, although the coast is primarily rocky. There are also some activities you may not have thought of, such as a place to see ospreys, the world's largest globe, and the state's original twenty-four-hour store, L. L. Bean.

Falmouth

Your first stop after Portland is **Falmouth,** a small, seaside community. Falmouth is worth a stop to visit **Mackworth Island.** Mackworth Island is only ten minutes north of Portland, but it is another world. Here you can hike, kayak, swim, or bike. The paths around the island offer spectacular views of Portland and the harbor. From Route 295 North, take Exit 9 for Route 1 North. On your right, you will see a sign for the Baxter School for the Deaf, which is on Mackworth Island. Turn here, and a small bridge brings you across to Mackworth Island.

A bit further up Route 1, but still in Falmouth, is **Gilsland Farm.** Gilsland Farm is well marked and will be on your left as you

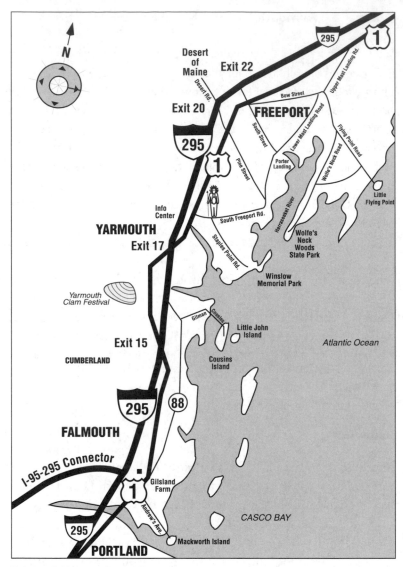

Falmouth, Yarmouth, and Freeport

While exploring this area, look for ospreys at Wolfe Neck Woods State Park, explore the mysterious Desert of Maine, enjoy the Yarmouth Clam Festival, and see Eartha the giant globe. *Map by Denise Brown of Ad-Cetera Graphics.*

head north. Gilsland Farm is a Maine Audubon Sanctuary offering good hiking trails, field trips, educational exhibits, and a gift shop. The Prescumpscott River runs past Gilsland Farm, offering good opportunities to see wildlife. Call (207) 781-2330 for more information. Gilsland Farm is open year-round.

Yarmouth

As you continue north on Route 1, you next will come to **Yarmouth,** another working seaport, and the former sardine capital of Maine. Royal River Sardines once were sold far and wide, but that enterprise has since moved on, although Yarmouth bustles with other trades. Founded in the 1630s, Yarmouth has long been known for its fisheries, shipbuilding, and for a time, its thriving papermaking industry. The success of many of these industries can be attributed to the Royal River and the power of its falls, which was harnessed for a variety of enterprises. The Royal River runs right through Yarmouth, as does Route 1. Today, Yarmouth has a diversified economy, with many small, successful businesses. Tourism, fishing, and lobstering all play important roles, while more modern enterprises such as furniture and map making have also made a name for themselves.

Most of the sites in Yarmouth are within easy reach of Route 1. A good place to start is the **Royal River Park,** with its picnic areas, riverfront trails, and views of waterfalls. Go left from Route 1 North onto Main Street and head west. Then, turn right onto East Elm Street and you will come to the park. The 40-acre park has wonderful walkways, launch areas for canoes and kayaks, and free summer concerts on Wednesday nights. The park is just off Main Street and either walking or biking is easy.

Another great place to explore is **Pratt's Brook Park,** which covers 200 acres of woods with more than 7 miles of trails for hiking or cross-country skiing. From Route 1 North, turn left onto East Main Street. Head north on East Main, then turn left onto North Road. The entrance to Pratts Brook Park is on your right on North Road.

If you are looking for a swim, drive out to **Sandy Point Beach**

on Cousin's Island. Yes, the beach is on an island, but it is accessible by car. This is a small, quiet beach with nice, white sand. The drop-off is gradual, so it is a good swimming beach for children. In season, there are temporary toilets but no other facilities. There is free parking nearby. You can reach Cousin's Island by picking up Route 88 on your right from Route 1 North, then turning right onto Gilman Road. Gilman Road will become Cousins Street, which brings you across the bridge and down onto the island. The beach is accessible year-round, but facilities are generally limited to the summer season, Memorial Day to Labor Day.

When driving around Yarmouth, you might notice cars slowing at the corner of Yankee Drive and East Main Street. (From Route 1 North, turn right onto East Main Street, which is also Route 88 East. Proceed east on East Main and you will come to the junction of Yankee Drive on your right.) Most likely they are stopping to pay tribute to **Herbie,** the biggest elm tree in New England. Herbie has graced this corner for centuries, and given the loss of so many of his kin to Dutch elm disease, the fact that he still stands is something of a marvel. Once, not that long ago, scores of New England towns had their streets lined with towering elms. The advent of Dutch elm disease, and its rapid spread, has greatly reduced the number of mature American Elms. Few American elms live to full growth before being stricken by the disease. Some tree owners inoculate their precious elms, but that cannot be done on a large scale. A new variety of American elm has been bred that is disease-resistant, but it is not the same great tree that was once so much a part of our community heritage. Hence, Herbie's fame.

Back on Route 1, be sure to stop at the **DeLorme Map Store.** As you head north on Route 1, the DeLorme map store is on your right; it is across from the Maine Tourism Association center—you cannot miss it. DeLorme has provided cutting-edge map products for the past twenty-five years. They produce paper atlases, award-winning mapping software, and other mapping technologies. Stop in to learn how maps are made and explore a wide range of mapping products, including a huge selection of print and software maps, globes, travel books and guides, global positioning systems (GPS), hand-held digital maps, gifts, toys, and more. Of course, you cannot visit the map store and not marvel at **"Eartha,"** the world's largest rotating globe. This extraordinary lit globe literally fills a huge section of the building. Eartha weighs 5,600 pounds with a total circumference of 130 feet! The globe is the largest printed image of our planet ever created. At DeLorme, they say "Visit Maine and See the World"—and they are right! The DeLorme Map store is open seven days a week. For more information, call (207) 846-7100 or visit **www.delorme.com.**

No one can visit Yarmouth and not try to catch the annual **Yarmouth Clam Festival.** Held each July, the festival is a family-fun-filled weekend with crafts, music, entertainment, and most important, lots and lots of clams. Clams are served in your favorite versions: steamed and fried, as cakes and in chowders. There is a huge parade, the famous diaper derby (a fun race for infant crawlers and toddlers), canoe races, and a clam-shucking contest. In 2004, the Festival also started featuring its butterfly house at Railroad Park. Walk through and watch two hundred delicate butterflies flit around you. The butterflies are released on Sunday; the house is part of an effort by a local greenhouse and farm to encourage gardening to support butterflies. Also at Railroad Park, see the "living statues" (humans dressed as a range of characters who stoically strike and hold positions for an amazing length of time) and hear a wide range of concerts, from doo-wop to barbershop. There is a huge "Pink Elephant" sale, free horse-drawn wagon rides, a Clam Festival postal cancellation, and a firemen's muster. Watch for Steamer, the festival's giant clam mascot, as he makes the rounds. The entire festival caps off with fireworks. For the date of this year's event, call (207) 846-3984 or visit **www.clamfestival.com.**

Freeport

After Yarmouth comes **Freeport** as you head north on Route 1. The Route 1 entrance to Freeport is marked by a 40-foot figure of a Native American (Route 1 is also Freeport's Main Street). Freeport is home to L. L. Bean, the king of the outdoor stores, as well as dozens of outlet shops and a wide range of parks. The community got its start with shipbuilding and shoe manufacturing, but while there is still a working harbor, retail is definitely the major industry.

To Mainers and those from away, Freeport is known primarily for one thing: **L. L. Bean.** L.L. Bean is a world-famous mail-order company and retail store. The company was founded in 1912 by Leon Leonwood Bean. For more than ninety years, L. L. Bean has been helping people of all ages enjoy the outdoors by offering durable, comfortable clothes and the finest in outdoor equipment. The store has a full kids department, called "L. L. Kids," full of everything a junior Maine Guide might need, plus some cool toys. In addition to an outstanding selection of outdoor and home goods, the store features a real trout pond, complete with waterfall. The store is open 365 days a year, 24 hours a day. Nearly everyone tries to shop L. L. Bean at least once at midnight or later—and no, the store will not be deserted! As you head north on Route 1, it will bring you right into downtown Freeport. L. L. Bean will be on your left—you cannot miss it.

In addition to great shopping, L. L. Bean offers a wide range of classes in the outdoor arts, many of them just for a day. Called the **Discovery School,** these classes include subjects such as kayaking, fly-casting, archery, and in winter, cross-country skiing and snow-shoeing. The classes can be a good way to introduce yourself to a new outdoor experience. Most classes are a half day to a full day, although some of the more in-depth fly fishing and kayaking classes can be two to three days. Most classes are at the introductory level, but a few advanced courses are available. If you think you and your family would be interested in sampling a Discovery School class, call in advance to inquire about what will be offered and reserve a space. Classes change with the seasons, and are popular, so space fills up quickly. The Discovery School is held at L. L. Bean. Call (888) 552-3261.

In summer, L. L. Bean's **Discovery Park** is home to a summer concert series. All concerts are free of charge and open to the public. Grab a picnic supper and a blanket and settle in for a relaxing evening. For this summer's schedule, call 1-800-341-4341. Discovery Park is on Route 1, on your left, just before L. L. Bean. Morse Street, on your left, will bring you into the park.

Surrounding L. L. Bean are **more than 100 outlet stores** of all types. In addition to world-class corporate outlet stores, there are antique shops, specialty shops, and craftsmen's boutiques. The shops are well laid out, so walking is easy. There is also a trolley service. Restaurants of all types are abundant, so it is easy to find a good place to eat and rest your feet. In addition to the chain fast-food restaurants, many smaller, privately owned eateries provide both speedy and economical family dining. Freeport is a shopping destination all year round, so expect crowds on weekends. Non-holiday weekdays from late fall through early spring are probably the quietest time.

The Freeport Merchants Association puts out an excellent map illustrating all of the stores and giving descriptions. The map also shows the location of restrooms, eateries, accommodations, banks, and parking. To make your outlet shopping as carefree as possible—especially with children in tow—stop by the Freeport Visitors Center. You may also call (800) 865-1994 to request a map before your trip, or visit **www.freeportusa.com.**

But Freeport isn't just about shopping. Here in Freeport is a real desert, a bizarre natural phenomenon created by erosion. Called the **Desert of Maine,** this intriguing attraction is worth a closer look. In 1797, the Tuttle family ran a 300-acre farm where the Desert of Maine now stands. They successfully raised crops of potatoes and hay for several years. However, they failed to rotate crops, and at the same time massively cleared the land and overgrazed their fields. The resulting severe erosion exposed the hidden desert. As the sand spread and spread, taking over their land, the Tuttles fled, leaving nature to her course.

The Desert of Maine. *Photo by Marcia Peverly.*

Geologists discovered that a glacier slid through this area about eleven thousand years ago, at the end of the last Ice Age, or Pleistocene Period. As the glacier carved its way across the land, it left behind the sand and mineral deposits that today make up the Desert of Maine. Scientists have documented that the desert is real. It does not have the flora, fauna, or climate of traditional deserts, but it is one nonetheless.

Trams take you on a guided tour through the shimmering sands where you will see a spring house completely buried by sand and other amazing sites. Later, you can walk about the desert on your own. This is a bizarre experience, as the sweeping sand dunes are surrounded by pine trees, blueberry bushes, and other typical Maine greenery. Kids will enjoy hunting for gemstones, making sand art, and visiting the farm museum. You can watch professional sand artists at work, as they create sand paintings and bottle designs.

The Desert of Maine has a gift shop, picnic area, restrooms, and convenience store, making it a fun and easy family outing. The attraction is open early May to mid-October, and is on Desert Road,

The Desert of Maine's buried spring house. *Photo by Marcia Peverly.*

which is just off both Route 1 and Interstate 95. From Route 1 North, Desert Road will be on your left, just after the Interstate 95 exit. For more information, call (207) 865-6962 or visit **www.desertof maine.com.**

Down by the water is Freeport's working harbor and **Atlantic Seal Cruises.** This cruise line offers all kinds of family-friendly outings. Set sail for a seal and osprey watch. Ospreys nest at nearby Wolfe's Neck Woods State Park (more information below). Take the Eagle Island adventure cruise, which brings you to the home of Admiral Peary, the first man to reach the North Pole. The cruise allows you to explore woodsy island trails, beachcomb, and watch for seals at various Casco Bay seal resting areas. There are also lobstering demonstrations on many cruises, special fall foliage trips, clambake trips, and even a Fourth of July Fireworks Cruise. Atlantic Seal Cruises departs from the Freeport town wharf daily from Memorial Day through mid-September. Fall foliage cruises run from mid-September through the end of October. For more information, call (207) 865-6112. Reservations are suggested. To reach the Freeport town wharf from downtown Freeport, take a right onto South Street and head east. South Street will become South Freeport Road and bring you to the waterfront. Once there, go left to access the wharves and harbor.

Freeport abounds with natural areas. Try climbing **Hedgehog Mountain,** which offers scenic, wooded trails for hiking, mountain biking, and cross-country skiing. Locals claim Hedgehog Mountain is "a piece of cake" to climb, and it certainly is a comfortable climb for children age six and up. Hedgehog Mountain is off Landfill Road. From Route 1 North, go left onto Mallet Drive. You'll then go left again and briefly be on Durham Road. Durham Road feeds into Pownal Road. Landfill Road is a left off of Pownal. *(Mark this page, as you will use these basic directions several times as you visit key sites in this area.)*

The Maine Audubon Society maintains **Mast Landing Sanctuary** on Upper Mast Landing Road, just off Route 1. Go right onto Bow Street from Route 1 North, then left onto Upper Mast Landing Road. This 150-acre sanctuary has easy walking nature trails, picnic areas, and great opportunities to see wildlife, especially birds. It is open year-round.

From Upper Mast Landing Road, return to Bow Street and head east; at the fork, take Flying Point Road on your right; then turn right onto Wolfe's Neck Road. This brings you down to **Wolfe's Neck Woods State Park.** Wolfe's Neck Woods is an outstanding ocean-front park with picnicking, restrooms, and nature trails. You can pick up a trail guide at the park. The trails are easy walking and lead through the woods and right along the rocky coast. Keep little ones in hand near the cliffs. Here the large pines that Maine is known for march right along the cliffs. The views of rocks, surf, and Casco Bay are spectacular. This is a classic glimpse of Maine.

Wolfe's Neck Woods is also known for its osprey nests. Ospreys or "fish hawks" are large, white hawks with black-banded wings that dive for fish. They are the largest eastern hawk, with a wingspan of up to 6 feet. They live in large nests, usually in a big pine near the sea or marshes, as they feed primarily on fish. They are amazing birds and watching one hunt and return to feed its young is awe-inspiring. If you are quiet, it is possible to see this at Wolfe's Neck Woods. For more information, call (207) 865-4465. Wolfe's Neck Woods is accessible year-round, although facilities will be limited after Labor Day, and not available come winter. If you come to the park in winter to cross-country ski, you may need to park outside the gate.

For a park with great swimming, visit **Winslow Park and Campground** on Staples Road. As you come into Freeport on Route 1, pick up South Freeport Road on your right. Staples Point Road, which leads to the water, will be a right off South Freeport Road. Winslow Park offers scenic waterfront camping (RV and tent), as well as daytime recreation. Here are the town beach, picnic areas, and nature trails. The park is perfect for families as all the amenities are available; the surf is gentle and the beach is sandy. If you tire of swimming, explore any of three unique nature trails, visit the playground, or just relax with a picnic lunch or supper and enjoy the view. There is also a cottage for rent at the park. Harb Cottage is available by the week in the summer season, and from November 1 through Memorial Day.

Although the park offers camping, day visitors are welcome, and only a small fee is charged. The park is open from 8:00 A.M. until 30 minutes after sunset. If you wish to book a campsite, the park season runs from Memorial Day weekend through Columbus Day, and rates vary. For more information about the park in general, or to reserve either a campsite or the cottage, call (207) 865-4198.

If you visit Freeport in the wintertime, watch for the **Holiday Sparkle,** a Christmas celebration running through the first two weeks in December. The Sparkle features a spectacular nighttime electric parade, carolers, open houses, concerts, free refreshments and carriage rides, and much more. Lodging will book up fast as folks descend on the outlets for their holiday shopping, so reserve accommodations early if you wish to attend.

After the holidays, Freeport and Falmouth celebrate **Maine Winterfest,** which features glittering sculptures of ice and snow, ice-carving demonstrations, sledding, skating, lots of hearty Maine food, merchant discounts, and more. For more information, visit **www.mainewinterfest.com.**

As you leave Freeport, consider a slight detour to visit the **Blueberry Pond Observatory** at 335 Libby Road in Pownal. Follow the directions for Hedgehog Mountain on page 120, but continue on Landfill Road until you come to Libby Road on your right. The Observatory carries you away on a guided tour of the stars. You will get to see the moon, stars, and planets through a 12-inch telescope. You can also take pictures of your favorite planet, nebula, or galaxy to take home! When folks ask you where you went on your vacation, show them these photos! Nighttime sessions are two hours long and are available for up to five people. This may be too long for younger children, but older ones will be fascinated by this window to the heavens. Reservations are required. For more information or to make a reservation, call (207) 688-4410 or visit **www.blue berryobservatory.com.**

While in Pownal, visit **Bradbury Mountain State Park.** The park offers camping, hiking, picnicking, and the chance to scale a 484-foot granite bluff, also known as Bradbury Mountain. The reward for getting to the top is a spectacular view of the surrounding countryside. Younger children may find this hike too strenuous, but older children, say age ten and up, will appreciate the view and the accomplishment. Bradbury Mountain is also an excellent place to cross-country ski or snowshoe in winter months. Like the other parks, you will find limited facilities after Labor Day, and no facilities come winter. Call (207) 688-4712 for more information. To reach Bradbury Mountain State Park, follow the directions for Hedgehog Mountain from Route 1, but stay on Pownal Road until you reach Route 9. Bradbury Mountain is off Route 9 and is plainly marked. There will also be signs for the park from Route 1 in downtown Freeport.

✍ How to Get the Most from a Nature Walk

People sometimes wonder why they don't see more animals when they go on a nature walk, but wildlife is all around. You simply have to look for clues and change your approach.

Choose the right time of day. Most birds and animals are more active in the early morning and early evening then midday.

Be quiet. Animals have keen hearing and can detect your approach long before you see them. All animals have enemies, and since humans are bigger than most animals, it is not surprising that they hide when they hear us coming. If you are quiet, stop, wait, and listen, you will see more than if you chatter and move about.

Listen. You will hear birds before you see them. Every bird species has its own distinctive song. Birds sing most in the early morning and late afternoon and evening. In the spring and early summer months, listen for the songs of spring frogs. Later in the summer, insects will trill the night away, and you may also hear the call of an owl in the night.

Look for clues on thorny thickets and barbed wire fences. You may find the hairs of foxes, deer, or rabbits caught there. Feathers are easy to find. If you find feathers or hair often in the same place, there may be a den or nest nearby, or you may be on a game trail. For example, white or reddish brown tufts of fur near a burrow in the ground may signal the home of a red fox; brown feathers with bands of black and tipped with white near a hollow log may mean the territory of a ruffed grouse. The male grouse "drum" on the hollow logs with their wings during the spring mating season. The air fanned by the wings makes a loud noise.

Check for nests and holes. The burrows of chipmunks and foxes are easy to see. The size of the burrow will give you a clue as to who made it. Look for signs that it is still occupied—are there food remains, droppings, or hairs? You may find some well-worn tracks leading away from the burrow. Some animals follow the same paths when they go out hunting for food.

Bird nests are easy to find. Note the size of the nest and what it is made of inside and outside. Are there any features to give you clues about what bird is nesting there?

Animals are untidy eaters. Many leave the remains of their food on the ground. Different animals feed in different ways. Squirrels split nutshells in half while voles gnaw a round hole through them. Dormice and voles leave a smooth edge to the hole, while wood mice leave teeth marks. Nuthatches and woodpeckers often wedge nuts in tree bark, either as a storage place, or to hold nuts firm while they hammer them open.

Look for tracks on the ground. Tracks are more easily found when the ground is soft or covered with snow. Good places to look are in the mud beside streams and ponds, in sandy areas, and in areas where the soil is not covered by vegetation. Note the size of the tracks, how many toe prints there are, and the distance between the tracks. Look at the detail of the tracks. Has the animal got long claws? Are its feet webbed? See if you can tell which tracks belong to the forefeet and which belong to the hind feet. Are there any other clues—feathers, hair, droppings? Have its wings or tail left their mark, too?

Watch for droppings. Animals leave behind their own characteristic droppings. The droppings of a dog or fox are different from the small pellets that rabbits and deer leave behind. Look for owl pellets—oblong rolls of fur with tiny bones inside. After eating a mouse or vole, the owl coughs up the part of its meal that it cannot digest. Foxes sometimes do this, too.

A good field guide can enhance your outdoor experience. Any of the Peterson Guides are excellent references, and Audubon offers a good selection as well. Both series offer guides to tracks, birds, animals, plants, and trees, to name a few.

Many of these same tips work well at the beach. You can look for bits of hair and fur on the wild roses and bramble bushes found along the shore. Songbirds nest here, too, so check for nests. At low tide, the clam flats (also called mud flats), are great for showing tracks. Bring a seashore guide or bird guide along, as this will help you identify the trails of marine animals such as clams and worms, and the footprints of shore birds. While sea and shore birds do not "sing" like the inland birds, they do fill the morning air with their cries and calls. A bird guide will give you an idea of who is "saying" what as you stroll the beach.

Whether inland or by the shore, if you come across a wild animal, do

NOT make an effort to touch it. Wild animals do not know that you mean them no harm. While their first instinct is to flee, if they feel cornered, are defending nearby young (which you may not see), or feel that you are a predator, they may bite or scratch. Any animal bite or scratch is dangerous, and would require a trip to the emergency room for tetanus shots. Wild animals can also carry rabies, a disease that can be fatal. If you come across a wild animal that is acting strangely—overly aggressive or unafraid—or looks ill (straggly coat, thin, possibly drooling or foaming at the mouth), steer clear. The animal could be ill with rabies. If you sight such an animal, tell the nearest park ranger, campground manager, game warden, or animal control officer. Rabies is more common among species such as raccoons, foxes, skunks, and the like, but even deer, rabbits, and birds can catch the disease—in fact, any warm-blooded animal can. For this reason, if you are traveling with pets, make sure they are up to date on their rabies immunizations and are wearing a tag that indicates this.

The wild animal warning applies to seals as well. It is not unusual to find a seal resting along the rocks or beach. Frequently, they are doing just that—enjoying a nap or the warmth of the sun. If the seal seems ill or in distress, tell the lifeguard (if there is one), or contact the marine patrol (any local hotel, shop, store or marina can assist you with this). Do not attempt to aid or touch the seal yourself. Often, baby seals are seen on the shore and folks attempt to "rescue" them. Usually, the mother simply has left the baby to rest while she hunts for food. If the baby seems ill, or no mother has returned after a day or so, then notify the marine patrol or other park or beach official.

Falmouth Highlights at a Glance

- Mackworth Island
- Gilsland Farm: (207) 781-2330
- Falmouth has no chamber of commerce; call Portland: (207) 772-5800

Yarmouth Highlights at a Glance

- Royal River Park
- Pratt's Brook Park
- Sandy Point Beach on Cousins Island
- Herbie, the giant elm
- Eartha, the giant globe at DeLorme's Map Store: (207) 846-7100
- Yarmouth Clam Festival: (207) 846-3984
- Yarmouth Chamber of Commerce: (207) 846-3984

Freeport Highlights at a Glance

- L. L. Bean: (800) 341-4341
- Discovery School: (888) 552-3261
- Discovery Park concerts: (800) 341-4341
- More than 100 outlet stores
- Desert of Maine: (207) 865-6962
- Atlantic Seal Cruises: (207) 865-6112
- Hedgehog Mountain
- Mast Landing Sanctuary
- Wolfe's Neck Woods State Park: (207) 865-4465
- Winslow Park
- Holiday Sparkle
- Maine Winterfest
- Blueberry Pond Observatory: (207) 688-4410
- Bradbury Mountain State Park: (207) 688-4712
- Freeport Visitors Center: (800) 865-1994

Take in an old-time agricultural fair or visit a family farm and pick some produce of your own. Eat some lobster, help catch some lobster, watch whales or sunsets. Test your skill at miniature golf, and come winter, head outdoors to cross-country ski, sled, or skate.

You can see **lobstering and eat lobsters** anywhere along the Maine coast, as lobstering, along with fishing and shipbuilding, are major parts of the coastal economy throughout the state. Similarly, you can go deep-sea fishing or find various cruises—both scenic and whale-watching—all along the coast. A few specific offerings are highlighted here and there, but every coastal community has lots of choices. The local chamber or visitor center will have a complete listing, or stop by any marina.

Miniature golfing is another activity that is found throughout the southern part of the state, with many fun courses. Kittery, Wells, and Old Orchard Beach are just a few of the towns with courses.

Even though the southern Maine coastal area is more developed than other parts of the state, thankfully there is still an abundance of **family farms.** As you drive through any of these communities, you will see farm stands and "pick-your-own" signs. If you want more specific listings, again, ask at the local chamber, town hall, or any local store. (Some of these produce stands and picking invitations can be spontaneous, based on an especially abundant crop, so going for a drive in the country can be as good a way as any to find a farm.) In the summer, many farms are open for picking strawberries, blueberries, and later, raspberries. In fall, watch for pumpkins and apples. Many local farms combine fall picking with hayrides, music, and other entertainment, and special refreshments.

Summer and fall are also the time of the **agricultural fairs.** Such fairs are held throughout the state. An agricultural fair is a wonderful American tradition. This is the time when farmers gather to show off their livestock and their crops. It's a celebration of the harvest—and of many months of hard work. Cattle, pigs, chickens, rabbits, and all manner of livestock are judged. Draft horses and oxen compete in pulling contests—hauling huge sledges a specified distance with ever-increasing weight. Whichever team can pull the heaviest load the farthest wins. Some fairs also hold tractor pulls, but the horses and oxen are the time-honored favorites.

Crafts, quilts, and baked goods vie for prizes, and are also up for sale. Many fairs offer popular contests from yesteryear, such as pig scrambles (Try catching a piglet with your bare hands!), sheep roundups (Try herding a flock of sheep!), corn-shucking contests (How fast can you strip the husk from an ear of corn?), and the like. Folks also gather to watch sheepdog demonstrations. It's amazing to see these clever canines (usually border collies) round up wayward sheep and move them at the farmer's whim. They may be asked to herd them to one side of the field or another, bring the sheep into an enclosure, or single out just one or two animals. The farmer uses only hand signals and whistles to command the dogs. The dogs rely primarily on their posture (usually a crouch or crouching walk), intimidating eye contact, and a few nips at the heels to move the sheep. Seeing a good farmer/collie team at work is like watching a silent ballet, as dog and man are in perfect harmony.

Today's fairs are also part carnival, with midways, rides, beauty pageants, and plenty of cotton candy, popcorn, and snow cones. You'll want to spend the day—and maybe an evening, too—as the fairground lights turn a simple field into something magical. Some of the fairs held in the southern section of Maine include:

- **Ossipee Valley Fair in South Hiram in July.** An old-fashioned fair with unique exhibit halls, lots of livestock, midway, drag racing, and animal pull events. Visit **www.ossipeevalleyfair.com**.
- **Topsham Fair in Topsham in August.** Great agricultural exhibits, animal pull events, 4-H, crafts, midway, and harness racing. (No web site—see general fair web site at end of this section.)
- **Acton Fair in Acton in August.** Outstanding exhibits, 4-H,

livestock exhibits, flower show, animal pull events, and midway. (No web site—see general web site at the end of this section.)
- **Cumberland Fair in Cumberland in September.** Large exhibit halls, midway and livestock exhibits, animal pull events, and harness racing. Visit **www.cumberlandfair.com.**
- **Fryeburg Fair held in early October.** Fryeburg is Maine's largest agricultural fair, and is known for its beautiful setting. Since the fair is usually held at the peak of foliage season, tourists flock to the event after viewing the region's spectacular autumn scenery. Fryeburg Fair has exhibit halls, a museum, harness racing, and livestock shows. Visit **www.fryeburgfair.com.**

All of these fairs feature agricultural displays of produce and livestock, entertainment, carnival rides, games, and lots of great food. For this year's fair schedule, visit **www.maineagriculturalfairs.org.** A brochure on the agricultural fairs and a listing of pick-your-own stands (not all inclusive) are available at the Maine Tourism Association off I-95 North and Route 1 in Kittery.

Come winter, cross-country skiing, sledding, snowshoeing, and skating are all popular pastimes in southern Maine. Most of the town and state parks mentioned in this book allow cross-country skiing and snowshoeing, as do many local farms and golf courses. Brochure-type information on cross-country skiing is very limited and primarily covers ski centers that are part of downhill resorts in the northern and western parts of the state. For local cross-country ski opportunities in southern Maine, your best bet is to ask at the town hall or sporting goods center of the town you are visiting. Most anywhere you can cross-country ski you can also snowshoe.

An Inland Sampler

While many of southern Maine's attractions hug the coastline, there are some great family outings if you head inland a bit.

From Route 1 (North or South) in Wells, take Route 109 West toward Sanford (or, if you are driving up Interstate 95, get off at the

Wells exit and take Route 109 West). In Sanford, a small mill town and farming community, you will find **Smitty's Cinema** on your right as you head into the downtown area. Smitty's shows first-run movies but with a twist: Families sit on the seats of old Lincoln Town cars and can eat supper while they watch the show. A range of food items are available, but classic burgers and hot dogs, and of course, popcorn, are the most popular fare. There are menus for kids, and Smitty's is open seven days a week. For more information, call (207) 490-0000. Smitty's is very popular, so if you wish to see a show, especially on a weekend, you may be wise to buy your tickets in advance.

Next up is **Willowbrook at Newfield.** To reach Newfield, take the Wells exit off Interstate 95, and again, take Route 109 West to the junction of Route 11. Continue west on Route 11. This will bring you into the small town of Newfield. Willowbrook is a nineteenth-century country village museum, and listed on the National Register of Historic Places. Willowbrook is a slice of yesteryear. It was created by Mr. D. F. King Sr., who wanted to capture this era and share it with future generations. Everything in Willowbrook is authentic. Stroll quiet streets free of "motor cars," and walk through the small shops of days gone by. You might want to linger in the Amos Straw Country Store, still stocked with items from more than one hundred years ago. This store was once Newfield's post office, and was a popular gathering place throughout its time. Folks stopped to warm themselves at the pot-bellied stove, have a cup of coffee, and gather community news. A game of checkers was always underway, and remains so.

There are thirty-seven historic sites in Willowbrook. Visit a sprawling farm of years ago, take your seat in the tiny school house, or see the old-time firehouse. Take in a collection of antique tractors, steam engines, and the Concord Coach. The one featured here is the second-oldest in existence, dating from 1849. It once ran passengers along mid-coast Maine prior to the Civil War. You will see an elegant Victorian parlor, a child's bedroom complete with toys, a typical kitchen, and a grand ballroom waiting for the dance to

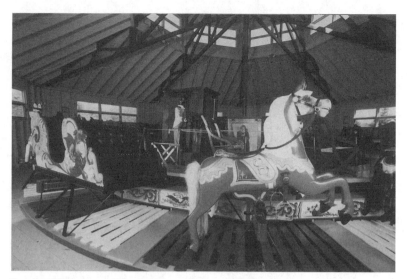

See the 1894 Armitage-Herschell Carousel at the Willowbrook Museum Village.
Photo courtesy of Willowbrook Museum Village.

begin. Children will be enchanted by the 1894 Armitage-Herschell Carousel, with its intricately detailed prancing horses. The carousel is operated three times a day, so you can see it in motion, but it is not available for rides save for one day a year. Each year, on the last Saturday before Willowbrook closes for the season, children are allowed to ride the classic carousel. This is usually the last Saturday in September or first Saturday in October. The web site posts the exact date each year.

Willowbrook is primarily a walking village, and little ones might find it overwhelming. Older children, however, should enjoy this walk into the past. No trip is complete without a stop at the Stable Restaurant and Ice Cream Parlor, or a visit to the Christmas Etcetera Gift Shop. There are restrooms on the premises and plenty of parking. Willowbrook is open daily from mid-May through September. There are special foliage season hours. Call (207) 793-2784 for more information, or visit **www.willowbrookmuseum.org**.

The **Harris Farm** in Dayton is worth a trip inland. You can reach the Harris Farm by taking the Kennebunk exit from Interstate 95, then Route 35 West. You can also pick up Route 35 West from downtown Kennebunk or Route 1. The Harris Farm is on Buzzell Road off Route 35. Harris Farm is a 500-acre working dairy and produce farm offering guided tours and hayrides through open meadows and sheltered woodlands. The second and third generations of the Harris family run the farm.

The fourth Sunday in July, the Harris Farm hosts "Lunch on the Land." Hayrides run continuously to the back meadow where a buffet picnic lunch, featuring farm-fresh foods such as their own hamburgers, corn, milk, salads, and desserts are served. The dairy barn is open for viewing and guided farm tours are available. Antique tractors are on display and fiddle music fills the air.

Come fall, the farm is a popular stop for picking pumpkins. The pumpkin patch is open Sundays from the end of September through October from 10:00 A.M. to 3:00 P.M. Hayrides to the pumpkin patch run continuously.

In the winter, the Harris Farm becomes a cross-country ski center, with skiing over numerous trails. There are 40-kilometer trails for novice, intermediate, and advanced skiers, skating lanes, and snowshoe trails. After skiing, stop by the lodge to warm up by the woodstove and enjoy the snack bar. Harris Farm also offers ski, snowshoe, pulk sled, and ice skate rentals, lessons, and a ski shop. (A pulk sled is a small sled for toddlers or infants. Parents pull the sled while they ski. The sled is attached by a long pole, about two ski lengths behind. This way, parents can get their exercise while the little ones enjoy a ride.) There is a fee for using the trails.

For more information on the Harris Farm or any of their events, call (207) 499-2678 or visit **www.harrisfarm.com**.

Just outside of Portland in Westbrook is **Smiling Hill Farm,** a working farm with plenty of child-friendly activities. There are pony and carriage rides, a petting farm, opportunities to help with feeding and milking, and most important, home-made ice cream! There is also a playground on the premises. In winter, Smiling Hill Farm is open for cross-country skiing and snowshoeing. Call (207) 775-4818 for more information. To reach Smiling Hill Farm, take Exit 46 off

Two lynx get playful at the Maine Wildlife Park. *Photo by Nate Barnes, courtesy of Maine Wildlife Park, Maine Department of Inland Fisheries and Wildlife.*

Interstate 95 North. At the stop sign at the end of the ramp, go left. You will come to a set of lights. From there, go left onto Route 22. Smiling Hill Farm is about 1.5 miles up on your right. Smiling Hill Farm is open year-round, seven days a week. Hours vary with the seasons, and according to special events, so visit **www.smilinghill.com**, or call (207) 775-4818.

From the Portland area, take Route 95 North to the Lewiston/Auburn area, then take Exit 63 for the town of Gray and Route 26 North. Gray is home to the **Maine Wildlife Park,** a wildlife facility run by the Maine Department of Inland Fisheries and Wildlife. It is a great place for children to be introduced to the native animals of Maine. More than twenty-five species of wildlife are featured, including white-tailed deer, moose, black bear, lynx, raccoons, fish, turtles, hawks, and owls. All the animals are unable to return to the wild, either due to injury or other factors.

There are nature trails, wildlife gardens, an education center, gift shop, picnic facilities, and "snack shack." Kids can have their

A black bear relaxes at the Maine Wildlife Park. *Photo by Nate Barnes, courtesy of Maine Wildlife Park, Maine Department of Inland Fisheries and Wildlife.*

pictures taken in giant black-bear cutouts and visit a fish hatchery. Throughout the summer, special events are offered on weekends.

The Maine Wildlife Park is open daily from mid-April through Veterans Day from 9:30 A.M. to 4:30 P.M. For more information, call (207) 657-4977 or visit **www.mefishwildlife.com**.

In this same area, head over to **Norlands Living History Center** in Livermore. From Interstate 95 North, take Exit 75 and head north on Route 4. From Route 4, turn right onto Route 108 East, then go left onto Norlands Road. Norlands is a 450-acre museum that takes you back to nineteenth-century small town life. Visitors assume the lives of people who once lived in the community and actively participate in farming, housework, and the political and social issues of the time. The living museum includes a library, Victorian mansion, one-room schoolhouse, farm, and other buildings. Visitors attend an 1870s church service and participate in other activities. On Wednesdays, Native Americans come to Norlands, bringing crafts and storytelling. Unique activities include over-

A "wild child" at the Maine Wildlife Park. *Photo by Mark Latti, courtesy of Maine Wildlife Park, Maine Department of Inland Fisheries and Wildlife.*

night adventures, monthly dinners, and barn dances. Special events are held throughout the year.

Norlands is open year-round, although hours vary with the seasons and according to special programs. Visit the web site or call the number listed below to confirm the hours for your visit. Reservations are required for tours in fall, winter, and spring, and preferred in summer, although drop-ins are welcome.

Norlands may not be for small children, but older children will be fascinated by this journey into another life. For more information, call (207) 897-4366 or visit **www.norlands.org**.

Southern Maine is a great destination for families, but all of Maine is yours to explore. The main thing about vacations is having fun. A great vacation leaves memories to last a lifetime. May your Maine vacation be one to remember!

🫐 *Blueberries*

Much of Maine's blueberry harvest is the wild blueberry, with its unique mixture of tartness and sweetness. About the size of a pearl, the Maine blueberry is an important part of Maine food, particularly in breakfasts and desserts. Look for blueberries on cereal, in pancakes, jam, syrup, and muffins, or as the star of blueberry pie, cake, and pudding. You might find blueberries sprinkled in your salad, and Maine berry farmers, ever creative, are now offering blueberry ice cream, salsa, dried blueberries, chocolate-covered blueberries (an unusual taste, but good!), and blueberry wine. Cultivated berries are larger and also very good eating, but they lack the tart flavor that characterizes the wild berries.

Bakers prize blueberries because, in addition to their delicious flavor, they hold their color and texture when baking. The growing season is short, but blueberries freeze well, so Mainers easily have blueberries year-round.

Maine produces more blueberries than anywhere else in the world. From mid-July until early September, blueberries can be found at scores of roadside farm stands, farmers' markets, and pick-your-own farms. Harvesting blueberries is back-breaking work, since much of it is still done using the traditional blueberry rake, which looks like a pronged dustpan. Wild blueberry bushes grow one year and fruit the next, so after the plants produce, the blueberry bushes are burned to the ground and the process starts again. (After a forest fire, blueberry bushes are one of the first shrubs to appear.)

Blueberries are very healthy, being rich in antioxidants. They may help the body fight cancer, heart disease, and aging. In addition, blueberries may improve motor skills and reverse short-term memory loss, help prevent urinary infections, and improve night vision. Want to know more? Visit **www.wildblueberries.com**. For some great blueberry recipes, visit **www.getrealmaine.com** or **www.wildblueberries.com**.

Inland Highlights at a Glance

- Smitty's Cinema: (207) 490-0000
- Willowbrook: (207) 793-2784
- Harris Farm: (207) 499-2678
- Smiling Hill Farm: (207) 775-4818
- Maine Wildlife Park: (207) 657-4977
- Norlands Living History Center: (207) 897-4366

Index